DEATH OF

THE GOLD

WATCH

To my father, a saint, who raised 3 daughters alone and worked hard to make sure we had the good shampoo, and more than once had to pee in the backyard because we were always in the bathroom. You taught the value of telling the truth no matter what and hard work. To my sister Jackie who kept me from giving up at least a dozen times in the early years of my business. To my mother, despite her demons, who gave me my strongest gifts; intelligence and intuition. This book is dedicated to you.

Table of Contents

Chapter 1: The New Workforce Landscape

"Choose a job you love, and you will never have to work a day in your life" ~ Confucius

We are in a new industrial revolution. And the key word here is "choice." The days of working for a company for twenty years and collecting the "gold watch" are all but gone. Things have changed radically since the "Great Recession." That recession wasn't so "great," anyway. It was a period during which entire professions were eliminated, mass layoffs occurred, and some of the world's most iconic financial institutions went bankrupt. The aftermath is that people don't trust big companies anymore as the only path to provide a living. The perceived "safety and stability" of working for a big company has shifted, and continues to shift, into something less stable and more unpredictable.

The ways of earning a living have changed radically with the gig and "sharing economy." It has created income streams where none existed before. It is providing people a way of earning money that did not exist with traditional employment. When I first started my company, and was working hard to get it up on its feet and generating income, I put the upper floor of my house on Airbnb and earned

$1,000+ per month to keep me going. I never would have had the opportunity for that alternative income stream ten years ago.

Why and how did we get here? What changed? And who's driving the shift? Is it corporations who want to cut costs and not pay benefits? That is what the politicians are saying. Is Uber destroying the traditional job structure? (Any NY taxi driver will have a strong opinion on this). Is it possible to make a living doing odd jobs on Task Rabbit? Can you really trust that babysitter or dog walker you found on Care.com? Is it "because of the millennials?" Notice that the word 'millennial' has become a catch-phrase for nearly everything. Perhaps this is because the group of people it refers to make up almost 50% of our workforce. I believe they are highly misunderstood. Although they did coin the phrase "side hustle," which is a cool way to explain the gig economy.

The reality is, we humans; your neighbors, friends, your former boss, former associates, or the kid down the street; are driving the change. This is not about the millennials alone. It is about us all. Despite the fact that this workforce doesn't offer the same benefits, and other "protections" provided by traditional employment, their numbers continue to increase. Why? Today, 38% of workers say they feel more comfortable working as an agile, or independent, employee than a perm employee.

The top three reasons, according to these employees, are "Flexibility of hours," "More control over my career," and "Pursuit of my passion" (in that order). According to the Randstad 2025 Workplace Report, by 2019 up to 50% of the workforce will be "agile."

The Workforce Model is changing and the Digital Revolution is a Big Factor.

We are in the digital age, with multi-functional devices connecting us. Brick and mortar offices are giving way to a remote workforce, co-working spaces, and flexible work hours. The 9:00-5:00 hour workweek is becoming obsolete.

According to Deloitte's 2017 Global Human Capital Trends, we are moving away from a full-time workforce and skill requirements. We are moving toward multiple workforces, with technologies defining delivery. The old style hierarchal (and let's face it, mostly patriarchal, but thankfully we are seeing changes there) style of leadership is on its way out. Gone, along with big mahogany desks and side bar of scotch and cigars. We are moving to a flexible organizational structure with more horizontal styles of leadership. Today, it's more about co-creating than managing. With artificial intelligence and data at workers' fingertips, more decisions will happen on the front line, where work occurs.

Some interesting trends are emerging as backlash to this outdated 'Traditional work" paradigm, besides the explosive growth of the gig workforce. *A growing number of young tech workers are expediting the path to financial independence by living frugally and following the "4% rule."* Zachary Crockett – Writer. They call themselves the "FIRE" community. Subscribers to the FIRE movement (short for "Financial Independence, Retire Early") don't feel like waiting around for the early bird special. Its concept is based on self-reliance, frugality, and smart investing as a path to financial liberation. The movement is nicknamed not "working for the man (or woman)" anymore.

The Way Work Gets Done has come a Long Way and the Gig Workforce is why.

The way we get work done has also undergone a major transformation. Companies today are moving to a more "fluid" workforce. This workforce is made up of full time, part time, as well as the catch all "gig economy." This later section of the workforce includes independent consultants, contractors, on-demand remote workers, and crowd-sourced employees. Crowd-sourced means a large group of people provided and engaged via the internet to complete projects. It also includes freelancers providing writing, design, and performance services for multiple companies.

A big enabler of this shift in how we get work done is Technology. Technology is your friend, embrace it. It is the delivery system for the majority of the gig workforce. We will go into more detail on this in chapter 8. In short, it is the delivery system and portal for you to access and onboard this dynamic workforce. The Technology explosion has been a critical factor in the dramatic changes in our workforce landscape.

Now that we have laid down some of the technical jargon, let's get to what this book is about; the *gig* workforce. Who they are, what they do, why they do it, and the companies that hire them. Most importantly, the workforce is made up of *People*. They are the lifeblood of your organization. The human race is shifting in how we view work; where we work, how we want to spend our time, and what we want out of work. We are shifting beyond looking at work as a means to an end; a paycheck, meetings, endless PowerPoint presentations, political maneuvering, mortgage, college tuition, one booze filled vacation a year in Mexico with the family, and at long last, retirement. If you saved enough, and are healthy enough, you live out the rest of your days on the golf course or traveling (if you are the top 15%). The rest get a part time job at Home Depot and downsize.

Not only has the workforce landscape changed, but so has the way corporations find, engage, retain and train their workforce. Currently, it is a "sellers" market for employment, with the workforce having the upper hand as talent becomes scarce, and boomers are leaving the workplace in droves. Organizations are seeking to embrace "alternative" workforce options and widen the net, to access talent, particularly in emerging skill set areas, such as manufacturing and technology (AI, Blockchain, Robotics). Manufacturing has an entire new industry emerging with computerization, automation and robotics. Some of the most progressive, and high-paying jobs are in manufacturing; despite the perceptions of low wages and menial jobs.

AI is not evil and will not replace the Human Race

Let's touch on the hot subject of AI, shall we? I don't believe it will create a super-race of machines that will wipe out the humans. I believe AI is a good thing. Yes, AI and robotics are permanently eliminating lower end jobs. It is also creating new jobs, at higher wages, that have a high demand for experience and skill sets that are not yet plentiful in the marketplace. This means competition and high wages for those that learned and have these skills. It's not replacing the role of The Humans, it's elevating us. It's creating jobs where we can best use our skills of creativity, engineering, and vision. Yes, it's putting some people out of work. It's eliminating entire job categories such as warehouse pickers, burger flippers, and repetitive tasks in manufacturing. A plant manager at a fortune 100 chemical company that was a former client of mine said "Robots never get tired, sick, or need a lunch break." I will say it was a wonder to behold shiny rows of robots picking up other shiny things and putting them in their shiny places. All in unison, and with precision. Before you vilify that manager, are those jobs the best use of the gifts, skills, and potential of "The Humans?" Is that a life, making forty thousand dollars a year and working a job standing on your feet all day, moving around the shiny things? Or is flipping burgers for ten dollar per hour? Or tracking lost shipments in a gigantic warehouse, walking up and down the warehouse the size of a baseball field finding lost inventory? Wait, that was my job in my early twenties, and I did it in heels and pencil skirt. I was transferred from the secretarial pool when they couldn't find me a position. It was brutal, and I was barely getting by, but I hung in there and gave it everything. My blue-collar heritage comes from my father, who worked in a steel mill most of his life. He raised me and two sisters on a steel workers salary, really good money in those days. But it was back breaking work, loud and dirty, and not temperature controlled. He worked hard to keep clothes on our back and food on the table, and some splurges now and then. He'd come home in the summer with his hair plastered to his head, worn out. He would sit down at the kitchen table; open a can of

Gennielight and look a little more at peace. At fifty-five he retired. That kind of work is hard on the body and, unless you are "in the office," hard to sustain. When I dropped out of college, my dad had me pick him up at work once and he took me around. I know now it was on purpose, he had a plan. My dad had a way of introducing things to his daughters that sunk in without us knowing what he was doing. He was brilliant at steering us in the right direction without ever feeling lectured (this is key when getting your teenage daughter to do what you want her to do). The steel mill was loud, dirty, hot and kind of scary. It was a kind of "scared-straight," hard labor style, to make sure I went back to college. It didn't work until fifteen years later. I did eventually finish my degree via night school, much later in life. At one point I was working two jobs and going to school part time. When I reflect back to the time, I realize how much easier it would have been if I could pick up a "side hustle" of my own in the gig economy. Perhaps, driving for Uber, or part-time coding. The hours and pay would have been better. Instead, I worked full-time as a financial analyst, and nights watching the clubhouse for an apartment complex for nine dollar per hour, and then studied at night.

Are We in a New Industrial Revolution?

Economists say we are in the middle of a new industrial revolution. Only this time, politicians and labor regulators are worried about the lack of benefits, and abuse of this population. The IRS, and federal and supreme courts are looking at "miss classification" of workers as independent contractors with gig employers like Uber, Amazon, and Lyft. The perception is that these companies have an unfair advantage over competitors who properly classify similar workers. A California Supreme court ruling in May 2018 has created a "seismic shift," which would limit businesses from classifying workers as independent contractors who aren't eligible for certain benefits. Similarly, employment protection was hailed as a big victory for labor and could shake up the state's so-called gig economy. In technical terms, the court put the burden on California employers to prove a worker is an independent contractor.

To do so, the company would have to pass each part of a three-prong test, known as the ABC standard, to prove a worker is an independent contractor. The test included that the worker is free of control and direction. The work is outside the course of business for which the work is performed, such as a plumber hired by a store to repair a leaky faucet, and the worker is engaged in an independently established trade or occupation. Will this ruling slow the explosive growth of the gig workforce and how they are engaged by employers? I don't believe so. I think this is the first of many shifts and repositioning of this 'New labor category' of workforce. It is the beginning of integrating this profile of workforce into society and embracing it, defining it, counting it, and ensuring this workforce is treated fairly. It won't slow the growth or usage of this workforce. It would just bring it into the light of day. The Bureau of Labor Statistics is only just beginning to get their arms around counting and accounting for this workforce. It is looking into their peculiar issues including where they work, who they are, what type of jobs they have. We have only begun to bring to light the depth and breadth of this workforce.

When you consider similar shifts in our workforce and labor, this is like the government passing the Factor Act in 1833 to improve conditions for children working in factories. Young children were working very long hours in workplaces, where conditions were often terrible. Today, employers must have an age certificate for their child workers.

Did the last industrial revolution stop children from working in factories and working long hours? No, it didn't stop children from working. It just regulated it and made it safer. The recent developments will not slow the use of gig workers. It would just moderate and regulate it. This is the way we work today. This is what we have chosen. We like the freedom, the flexibility, and we like having alternative ways to make money while we are looking for a permanent job. It's not perfect. There is wage inequality (despite the marketplace itself being neutral). There are workers who cannot make a living at the lower end of the pay scale in the gig workforce. There is work to be done, to be sure, but we have choices today for income streams that did not exist before. And given the growth of this workforce (despite low unemployment numbers) we see it as viable.

The Gig Economy provides Competitive Advantage

The politicians are right. The gig economy provides competitive advantages for companies today.

Per Praneeth Patlola – V.P. Products and Innovation at Compunnel said "The rising gig economy and workers mind shift with a preference towards flexible work is changing the way large enterprises acquire temp talent and no longer treat it just as a procurement function dependent on a pool of suppliers rather adopt direct sourcing models to use all avenues of talent sourcing."

Leveraging this workforce allows companies to be innovative, nimble, to bring in talent as needed, for as long as needed, and to align with the way we get work done. To take this to a broader view of how we work, this "Liquid Workforce," (a term first coined by Accenture), is made up of traditional employees and a wide variety of non-employee workers. This includes temporary workers, independent contractors/consultants/ freelancers, volunteers, outsourced resources, and even non-human options such as robots, drones, and cognitive computing applications. In other words, there is room for everyone; however you want to work, in whatever capacity.

This workforce allows companies to optimize competitive performance, to react to fluctuating markets and demand, as well as balance labor costs and workforce agility. The ideal state for any organization is finding the right combination of permanent employees, freelancers, and technology to ensure growth and productivity. We have had many clients in this category that we have helped navigate those decisions, to build the best workforce strategy for them, and implement the right processes and technology to get them there.

This "fluidity" allow companies to win by focusing on workplace innovation, and viewing their people as a strategic differentiator. The lines are being blurred between permanent, contingent, IC, cloud and crowd sourcing. Leading companies are using collaboration tools and cloud-based workflows that empower working at any time, and anywhere. This is not a trend being inflicted on workers. This is an EVOLUTION, or maybe a REVOLUTION. It is beyond an outdated, patriarchal way of working. There is the political backlash we discussed, and the cry for "benefits" and "protections" for workers who are participating in the gig economy. There are other options today that are cropping up for these workers; Per Jeff Oldham, SVP for Benefitfocus (a technology and services company that provides portable benefits to gig workers) "In America's 5 generational workforce, the need to offer a diverse set of benefits is critical in recruiting and growing the gig economy workforce."

As someone who worked as an executive for corporate America for twenty years, was fired twice, then became an independent consultant, and then headed up a consulting company, I now feel safer (and making more money) being on my own. The impartial market determined my income, and the marketability of my skill set and experience, and that of my consultants, is my safety and stability. I could never be fired again. I got my own benefits (for not much more per month than I paid when I had medical benefits through my previous companies). I feel more fulfilled, more excited, and feel like the sky's the limit now that I am heading my own company, as a consumer and contributor, in the gig economy. We "walk the talk" as gig economy advocates. We have no full-time employees, and all of our talent is an ecosystem of independent consultants. Most of them with their own consulting companies. This includes our lawyers, accountants, web designers, admin support, and various consultants across the gamut of experience and skill level.

Per a Forbes Jan 2018 Article, "This CEO predicts we'll see $1 billion-dollar company with only one employee by 2025." "Soon, one founder will be able to outsource every aspect of their company, and obtain sustained success without a single full-time hire," claims Roger Dickey, founder and CEO of Gigster, a San Francisco-based company that allows users to get tech projects built on demand. Dickey envisions a future where automation and intelligence tools will become more accessible and affordable in every industry. This would allow more entrepreneurs to run a successful company, and create innovative products, that won't be limited to firms with in-house talent.

Why this Shift Now?

Why this change in how, where, and why we work? "It's the millennials" is the catch-all phrase. And they do work differently. The few that I know, and have had the pleasure of working with, are bright, creative, and want to be inspired and have true leadership and mentorship. And they will call you on it if you don't provide the leadership and mentorship they need to perform. Maybe that's not a bad thing. Maybe it's a good thing we are being held accountable. We also have Baby Boomers leaving the workforce; roughly 10,000 every day. This is leaving substantial talent gaps, due to the level of experience, and skills, walking out the door with them. In fact, the over-fifty set is some of the most highly sought-after talent today, due to their experience and expertise. The profile of our existing workforce has changed. What they want, why they work, and where they work has changed. We don't want to give our entire soul to a company doing something we hate for forty years. We want to enjoy our kids, have the flexibility to attend their school plays, work from home on snow days, or any day for that matter. An average workday could be working part time at UPS, then driving Uber and Lyft on the weekends (got this from profile of an actual Uber driver I met; Martin, awesome guy). In fact, some of my best insights in the gig economy have come from Uber drivers. Not very scientific, but insightful. Almost all said they liked the freedom and flexibility it gave them. So much so, they would forgo less overall income. Only one said they wish Uber provided benefits and planned on getting a "real job soon." One female Uber driver spoke about how she could just jump in her car whenever she needed extra money for her daughter, and save for a vacation. Many were former entrepreneurs themselves. In fact, some of my best business ideas came from the hundreds of trips I have taken with Uber over the past several years. (Don't tell my business coach). I gave up my car last year, as part of an experiment, and to "walk the talk." Could I rely on the sharing economy to get around, and "reduce my carbon footprint?" Yes, I love saying that out loud when I want to impress someone younger than me. It turns out it's cheaper and easier to use Uber. I can get more work done, and I am contributing to someone else's income. I also have a 4.9 Uber rating which I am ridiculously proud of.

The workforce landscape is a living, changing organism. It's made of businesses that employ, and leverage this workforce; technology, regulatory bodies, legal entities, state, and federal agencies. Most of all, it's made up of people who want different things than they did fifty years ago, and who have different reasons for working, including where and why they work.

The Gig Economy is evolving organically on its own because it works for both sides of the equation; the workers who participate, and the companies who want to be agile, innovative, and provide a working environment that suits every worker, whether they are perm, independent, part-time, or contract.

This shift has created a dynamic that has radically changed the employer/employee relationship. It's changed the way we find, source, retain workers, and get work done. All bets are off regarding employee loyalty to big corporations and the 'safety and stability" big enterprise organizations have promised for years. No one cares if they get a gold watch at the end of a thirty-five year stint, because they probably won't be there that long.

Chapter 2: Radical Changes to the Employer/Employee Relationship

"Choose a job you love and you will never have to work a day in your life." ~author unknown

---

The housing market crashed and shortly after, half-finished homes were lying dormant. Weeds began growing up through the cement foundations in abandoned housing developments and shopping malls. There are so many theories about what caused the great recession of 2008. In short, it was the bursting of the housing bubble, and home prices plummeted. People defaulted on the subprime mortgages they were given, that they couldn't afford in the first place. Mortgage backed securities fell, and the financial institutions that placed their bets on them crumbled. Okay, that's kind of how I understand it. Maybe we should just call it good old-fashioned greed and ego. Is that too simplistic? Possibly, but taking the Occam's razor approach, sometimes the simplest answer is the right answer.

The Great Recession, (*I know what you're thinking, why is it called that? There was nothing great about it...*), changed the agreement. All bets are now off regarding employee loyalty to big corporations and the "safety and stability" big enterprise organizations have promised for years. By the end of 2008, there were total job losses at 2.6 million or the highest level in more than six decades. CNN Money called it "Worst Year for Jobs since '45". *"We're seeing a complete unraveling of the labor market and are on track for getting beyond 10% unemployment,"* said Lawrence Mishel, president of the Economic Policy Institute. Entire job categories were wiped out for good. For example, when was the last time you met a travel agent or spoke to someone's "admin assistant" to set up a meeting? Okay with anyone under the age of fifty?

The Change Begins with the Employer/Employee Relationship

The aftermath of the Great Recession even changed the way people felt about job stability and working for a big corporation. Getting the big job, the office, with a fortune 100/500 lost some of its appeal. There were many people who "did everything right." "They got the college degree, worked hard to move up the ladder, delivered above and beyond what their performance review and sales plan dictated, and were still let go. Smart, talented, hardworking people get fired all the time, sometimes for lack of performance or poor job fit. But more often than not, it's for factors beyond their control; the economy, shifting customer preferences, a drop in stock price and "keeping the shareholders" happy. The Great Recession is a *larger than life* example of that.

Despite the fact we are now at the lowest unemployment rate in almost twenty years, (No Trump, you can't take full credit for that), it does not take into account those workers that permanently left the job market. It also fails to include those working part-time because that's all they can find with their current skill set, or their jobs were permanently eliminated from the workforce marketplace.

Companies had to make massive cuts and reduce their workforce to stay alive. They were not prepared for these types of cuts on such a massive scale. It's brutal to sit across from someone you've worked with for 20+ years and tell them it's over. These cuts, on this scale, left a scar in the human psyche. The way people viewed the need for permanent jobs in big companies changed forever.

Where do these workers go? To work for another company? Is there another way? The ebbs and flow of business, including changing markets, global pressure, recessions, changing customer tastes, create a dynamic that make it almost impossible to promise a job for twenty years. And maybe that's not a bad thing.

Controlling your own marketability and income can be freeing (and scary for many). It puts the worker back in the driver's seat, and the corporations benefit from a workforce that is 'fluid" and can adapt to the ups and downs of business and workforce fluctuations. Maybe if you embrace that "instability," rather than be surprised by it, and work with it, everyone comes out better in the end.

Enter the gig economy.

Today there are multiple ways to earn a living that did not exist before because of the gig economy. You have the sharing economy in which you can earn money by such activities as renting out your house, your car, or designer purse. You can put your handyman skills to good use on task rabbit and you can help design a new logo or edit someone's video on Fiverr. The point is that you have ways of making money that did not exist before. Can you make a full time living at it? It depends on how strategically you use these opportunities and market yourself. I met a peculiar driver through Uber who had a prison record; albeit fifteen years ago, and many companies would not give him a job. Uber did, and he made seventy thousand dollars a year and was proud of his 4.9 Uber rating and over five thousand trips. He drove fifteen hours a day some days, but he was proud of what he accomplished. He had the freedom, flexibility and an income stream available to him that did not exist ten years ago.

A few weeks ago, the Department of Labor released the results of its first contingent workforce survey. And well, they are wrong. Yes, that's right; I said the government is inaccurate and incorrect. And guess what, they admitted it just this week. The government was making the right effort but asking the wrong questions. The survey states the number of "alternative workers" is actually down from the numbers in 2005. Headlines like CNN's riff on this: "Gig Economy Jobs aren't really taking over American Workforce," from June 2018 are perpetuating this inaccurate assessment. For decades, the BLS has tried to count all the workers participating in the "alternative workforce." Given this is the first pass at the numbers; it was to be expected there would be some misses. The survey did not account for fifty-seven percent of workers on gig workforce platforms like Toptal, and Freelancer.com who consider themselves "employees." They were not counted. This workforce alone is estimated to account for over twenty-five percent of our total workforce.

Just this week, according to Bloomberg, Senate appropriators are urging the Bureau of Labor Statistics to change how it collects data so it has a clearer picture of the gig economy and advances in technology.

The Senate appropriations committee recently approved funding legislation (S. 3158) for the Labor and

Health and Human Services departments, teeing up the bill for full Senate consideration in the coming weeks.

The committee report stated that the proposal suggests a slight increase in funding for the Labor Department's BLS. It also offers suggestions for how the agency should continue gathering data on the gig economy and it recommended that the BLS should explore how technology, like artificial intelligence, is affecting the workforce.

Is this conflict in the data everyone's way of "keeping things the same," by denying the fact that the gig workforce is here, and the way we work has changed? Or is it just an antiquated survey method deployed by the Government? The paradigms we upheld for so long; go to college, get a good job, work your way up, and retire are shifting. The reality is that things have changed, we've changed. Maybe we want something else; more time with our families, work schedules that align with the way we live today, flexibility and freedom. How do we accommodate this shift, and how does that change the employer/employee relationship? It does change it, radically. It starts with the growth of the gig economy; with our workforce choosing independence.

What Was The Genesis Of The Gig Economy?

What started this fantastic growth of the gig economy, seemingly out of nowhere? And who started it? Was it the gig workforce tech companies, swimming in piles of VC capital who had to justify their existence? It's not been a *"build it and they will come"* scenario. These technology companies are responding to a shift in how we procure talent and how the talent wants to, or possibly has to, work today. They are responding to a growing need and interest in embracing multiple avenues to supply talent and ways of getting work done. There are growing numbers of workers participating in these talent communities and getting work this way. But where did it all start? What was the genesis?

According to Talent Tech Labs, a talent technology incubator company based in NYC, that investigates, researches, validates, and accelerates emerging Talent Acquisition Technologies; technology has been the biggest instigator when it comes to the influx of Gig Work and the conversation that surrounds it. Businesses like Uber and Door Dash established a whole new approach to employment. Their models allow individual workers to make their own schedule and work as many hours as desired under the classification of an independent contractor. *"The gig economy is a term that refers to the increased tendency for businesses to hire independent contractors and short-term workers, and the increased availability of workers for these short-term arrangements."(Larry Alton, January 24, 2018, Why the Gig Economy Is the Best and Worst Development for Workers under 30, Forbes.com)* The reality is, because more businesses are embracing using the gig economy, enabled by this technology (the talent technology), there are escalating new entrants in the talent technology and gig workforce market. On-demand labor platforms, career advice and coaching, referral tools, job search organizers, temporary labor marketplaces, recruitment marketplaces, candidate relationship management, interview management tools, video interviewing, behavioral assessment, analytics, vendor management systems, and freelance management systems are just a few examples of the technology explosion that is helping companies source, vet, connect and on-board the best and brightest talent. Many of these technology companies and tools deploy machine learning and AI to enable the most efficient results. Human Resource leaders continue to struggle to keep up with the trends, but it would behoove them to do so. Leveraging this technology will be a competitive differentiator.

The 2008 Recession changed the perception of full time employment as a safe and stable place. Then enter the millennials who desire flexibility and independence. And they want to work with companies whose values align with their own. Working as an independent contractor in a gig economy gives them more control over the work they do, and their careers overall, helping them build career independence. They are not looking for a handout, or easy ride. They are motivated differently. Maybe we should do a better job of understanding them as they will be fifty percent of our workforce in a couple of years. They redefine loyalty — they won't stay if they are not engaged. Maybe that trumps the twenty- year veteran who really stopped trying somewhere along the twelve-year mark, but didn't tell you. This signals another shift in the employer/employee relationship.

So, what created this explosion in the gig workforce and the way we work? Was it technology, the Great Recession, the aging out of the baby boomers, or the growth of the millennials? Was it a growing distrust with Corporate America and the "stable job?" I think it is a natural result of major shifts in how we want to live, work and play. The technology explosion is a natural byproduct, not the other way around. Like a sort of *Darwinism* and *survival of the fittest*. Darwinism by definition is a theory of biological evolution developed by the English naturalist Charles Darwin (1809–1882) and others, stating that all species of organisms arise and develop through the natural selection of small, inherited variations that increase the individual's ability to compete, survive, and reproduce. The Gig Economy is a natural evolution of how we work and other factors that have created a shift in the "ecosystem."

How we work has changed, permanently.

The "variations" that are creating these shifts in how we work, and how companies are procuring and leveraging talent are a result of several occurrences. The Great Recession created a ripple effect in how we view work, the workplace and how and where we want to spend our time. The age-old paradigms of top down, patriarch management are crumbling to a new way of getting work done. Organizations are becoming flatter, leveraging networks and teams to get work done. We are also seeing a movement in regard to the traditional "patriarchal" structure within most companies. The #METoo movement and "peeling back" of the long standing male dominance in the traditional business world is shifting. As millennials enter the workforce, they are responding to more "feminine" leadership qualities; creativity, collaboration, and empathy. We are seeing more articles written about the "power empath" and "loving" your employees. This shift could be a response to some of the distrust generated for big enterprise during the great recession. It could be a response too to the distrust generated for a model of corporate leadership that is no longer relevant. These factors are permanently changing the way we work.

Market demand changes on a dime and having a fluid workforce to accommodate these changes works for both sides of the equation. Both sides benefit. Marry that with a workforce that is moving towards flexibility and freedom. You now have a different agreement between the employer and "employee." The gig economy is not being inflicted on the masses. Companies are not leveraging gig workers to get out of paying benefits or to shortchange the worker in some way. For the first time in a long time, the focus is back on the worker, the "humans". The worker is back in the driver seat, and after the Great Recession, they want to stay there. Even if it means striking out on their own, taking the risks of becoming independent, and ensuring their own marketability. This shift in how, where and why we work is the genesis of the changes. If you don't believe me, take the next five rides with any Uber Driver and ask them why they drive Uber. Ask them if they feel "shortchanged" in some way by lack of benefits, etc. Not very scientific, but the responses will be enlightening, trust me.

With the experienced baby boomers leaving the workforce, companies are scrambling to find talent in record low unemployment. Talent has become a #1 priority for many leaders. Not just how to find them, but how to keep them, inspire them, train them, and get the most out of them. It's not enough today to just "give someone a job and fair pay." We are now looking at talent and workforce strategy in radical new ways and for many companies the "struggle is real" to adapt to this new normal. Traditional sourcing and recruiting models are outdated. This includes finding candidates, reviewing resumes, and conducting multiple interviews over a period of weeks. This means you may lose that candidate to another company who uses the AI and Technology referenced earlier. This can reduce the hiring timeline to less than a week.

With unemployment low, companies who are looking to hire the best and brightest are finding unique ways to attract candidates; free yoga, craft beer Fridays, signing bonus, and nap rooms are just a few (and not just in Silicon Valley). Companies are also leveraging Brand Ambassadors. They typically promote a memorable experience related to your organization's brand. In the case of candidate experience, you could include previous candidates, new hires, and tenured employees in your interview process to not only evaluate the candidate, but also sell the opportunity through a lens that resonates with them.

This goes deeper than free yoga and dry cleaning. Candidates hear it from your employees, the people building your company. Companies such as Yelp, Hollister, and Sonic Automotive have successfully implemented Brand Ambassador Programs. They are using internal initiatives and external marketing efforts to leverage the real-life social networks of their customers and employees to better gain market share.

Now that the relationship has changed, how do companies adjust? It requires a radical change in thinking, and how talent is sourced, retained and leveraged. It's about providing those workers, who want flexibility and control over their own income and career path, an opportunity to contribute to your organization as a "non-traditional" resource. They may want to work remotely, may live in another country and some you may never meet. How does that work? Can this worker contribute in the same way as a permanent employee? Will they care enough about the company culture and fit in? Maybe the question is, will they contribute meaningful work, provide a different perspective, and help your organization meet its objectives? Maybe you will never see them around the water cooler or break room. But technology, social media, workspace applications, and Skype make it easier than ever to connect, and have group meetings. For a generation that grew up connecting via social media and their phones, this technology approach to stay "connected" may feel more real than seeing someone at the water cooler. In many ways, working as a gig or independent worker creates a bigger incentive to perform because your marketability and billable hours depends on it. Unlike in large organizations where mediocrity can hide and thrive for years, that is not the case for the independent workers. Your ability to earn a living is tied directly to your marketable skill sets and what you can deliver for an organization.

This is not just a change in thinking for Human Resources and Talent Acquisition. It impacts all divisions within a company. The promise of a steady paycheck is no longer enough. And history has proven that "steady" is a term used loosely in today's volatile economic climate. A gold watch at the end of a long career is not the goal for most of this generation. Most workers today won't be at a company long enough to collect it.

So how do companies adapt to the new workforce landscape? How do they integrate this workforce into their overall workforce strategy, to work side by side with their permanent talent? How do companies find, source, leverage the technology, and accommodate the regulatory and compliance requirements for engaging an independent workforce?

Workforce planning strategies that do not accommodate gig workers will not succeed. Some of your best talent can ONLY be found in these gig workforce communities because that is the way they WANT to work.

So the question is, how do organizations today adapt and accommodate this new workforce? Where do these workers fit in alongside "traditional talent?" Recently there has been a lot of buzz around legislation making it more difficult to use independent and "nontraditional" workers. How do organizations make room for this new breed of workers? How do we balance flexibility in how and where we work, with security of social rights? Something to ponder in the gig economy.

These are questions we hear and answer often. In the next chapter, I will share some of the best practices for engaging this growing and highly-skilled workforce. These practices ensure success for the workforce and the companies who engage them.

Chapter 3: Workforce Strategy – New Paradigm

"There is nothing permanent except change." ~ Heraclitus

Any large organization needs a talented, skilled workforce to thrive and grow. It's a deal breaker. Today, companies are challenged in adapting to the new workforce landscape, and navigating how to integrate independent consultants, gig workers, contractors, and part-timers into their workforce planning that traditionally focused on permanent hiring. Use of contractors and independent consultants, ten years ago was more of a ""fill in", or to accommodate seasonal shifts in demand like in manufacturing, or to provide short term support for projects, "outside" specialized expertise, or a "test run" for permanent hires. Contractors and independent consultants were ancillary and "outside" the "true" workforce.

"I've been in the freelancing consulting field from the get go, and I see more and more industries adopting and evolving the gig economy: taxi driver, education consultant, realtor, financial professionals. If you are not embracing gig economy yourself, you have already been surrounded by it. Subcontracting/freelancing has been the norm in many specialty service industries. Knowledge is not power until it's been applied and gig economy is the most efficient way to spread knowledge and make a bigger impact." Says Tony Zhang – Intendent Consultant and Fellow Charlotte Chinese Chamber member.

Today the lines are blurred and the workforce is more fluid, with some organizations having as much as fifty percent or more of their organization made up on non-traditional labor. Now it's just about talent; the best talent, procured as quickly as possible, the fewer steps the better. What form that talent takes and in what roles they best serve is the challenge. The perception that permanent talent is the best option, where you will have the highest quality, engaged workforce is outdated. Some companies are catching up to this shift slowly, but if they are to compete in a dynamic market, they will need to embrace multiple channels of talent to stay competitive and have a strategy to engage those channels in a way that is seamless and effective. Marry that need with the wide range of HRIS and talent technology options, staffing providers, gig workforce platforms, AI, couple with shifting risk and regulatory requirements around using non-traditional talent, and you have a layer of complexity that did not exist before. Gone are the days when you see an ad in the help wanted section (preferably at a cool and trendy coffee shop) and show up on time in your best suit and resume in hand. Okay, well some of that is true; the best suit part (or khakis and kicks if it's that kind of company), that tip will never go out of style. Today your next worker could be delivered via an on-demand talent cloud platform and you may never meet them in person. They may never make it to your waiting room and instead may be interviewed over video, discovered by bots scanning LinkedIn and their social media. The sourcing, delivery, vetting and interviewing methods are all being disrupted by technology.

This adds to the complexity; this development of the "new normal" for the workforce landscape is a relatively new one. Old models of workforce sourcing, vetting, on boarding, are still at play. The workforce that is part of the Gig Economy is already better educated on their options on how to make a living this way. Uber drivers have systems to maximize their earnings while maintaining other full or part time work. Independent Consultants are savvy marketers of their skills and brand and their talent will go to the highest bidder while they do the kind of work they enjoy for as long (or as little) as they enjoy.

Where organizations are challenged is in the volume of options available; "there are too many choices; one company will provide gig workers, another one will provide that plus risk mitigation, another one includes that plus IC invoicing"; it's too much. Ease of use is key. But we are at an inflection point for the shift." Says Thespina Spivey, Contingent Workforce Director for Coca Cola. That about sums it up. Companies recognize the opportunities to access this talent; but big ships move slowly. Moving away from the traditional model of hiring which is mostly permanent talent and accepting that a large population of their workforce will need to come from non-traditional labor sources is a big shift. Not just from a process standpoint but embracing the fact that some of the most qualified and skilled talent will only be found in these communities. I remember a conversation I had with a high level HR executive at a large fortune 100 food services company three years ago. We had been talking to them for a few weeks and got into it as far as what they wanted to do with their contingent workforce and how we could help optimize that workforce, drive quality and performance, provide visibility, etc. The HR Executive bluntly stated they "want to move away from contractors" as the staffing suppliers who provide them are "bottom feeders" and "you won't find the best talent that way." They wanted to reduce their contract labor and their reliance on it. In their minds, the best talent came from a permanent workforce who will be "more loyal" and 'better skilled" than a "body shop" providing contractors who are just biding their time till they can find a permanent job. It's a limiting belief and one that could hurt a company in the long run.

This week the NY Times posted an article: *"Paychecks Lag as Profits Soar, and Prices Erode Wage Gains"*.

The article highlights how corporate profits have soared but wages gains have not caught up. Businesses have been more successful at regaining losses from the downturn. Since the recession ended in 2009, corporate profits have grown at an annualized rate of 6.5 percent. Yearly wage growth has yet to hit 3 percent. Businesses may not have caught up with the new market; where today the worker has the upper hand as unemployment's slips below three percent for professional and educated workers. Gone are the days post the Great Recession where workers were grateful to get a paycheck at all.

Economists have offered various explanations for why workers are not doing better: the steady weakening of labor unions, the ability of American companies to find cheaper labor abroad or automate further, piddling productivity growth and the rise of superstar companies that are extremely efficient with a relatively small labor force.

The article stated the growing use of "Independent Contractors" puts workers at a disadvantage. But it begs the question, are the Independent Contractor workers also a willing participant? Maybe the shift is not being driven by big business; but it's a response to the changes in how we work? Automation and AI has made it possible for companies to operate more efficiently. Workers are no longer beholden to a traditional employment model.

Maybe this trend combined with the massive layoffs and mercurial decisions by companies to hire and fire at will are changing the employer-employee relationship.

Inc. published an article called: "What Is Employee 'ghosting'? How Companies Created Their Own Worst Nightmare." In fields ranging from food service to finance, recruiters and hiring managers say a tightening job market and a sustained labor shortage have contributed to a surge in professionals abruptly cutting off contact and turning silent--the type of behavior more often associated with online dating than office life," writes LinkedIn's Chip Cutter. A job candidate may agree to an interview and never show up. Or they may go so far as to accept a job, yet never appear for the first day of work. And the behavior isn't limited to candidates; companies have increasingly reported stories of employees who simply leave and never return, no formal resignation, no explanation given. Kind of like that really cute guy (or girl) you were so SURE would call... or you dated steadily for a couple months then just disappears.

Maybe it's the effects technology has had on the communication style of younger generations. Social media and messaging apps have helped persons establish relationships quicker, but a lack of face-to-face conversation and personal contact often make for relationships that lack depth.

Simply put, many feel no need to have an awkward conversation with a recruiter or manager if they can take the easy way out and ghost them. Or as the article states "They're simply getting a taste of their own medicine." Ouch.

Maybe it's backlash for years of a model where the employer had the power. "Let's remember that employers ghost their employees all the time," stated one LinkedIn commenter. "Have you ever worked at a company where management decided to lay off thirty percent of the workforce so they could hit the numbers to earn their bonuses? Employees find out on Friday afternoon that they won't be allowed inside the building on Monday morning... 'At will' employment is a brutal arrangement in which employees can quit at any time for any reason and employers can fire employees at any time for any reason. Hate the game, not the players."

Ghosting isn't respectful and could be a sign of future behavior so cut your losses while you can. Same thing for that guy (or girl) by the way who disappeared after a couple months.

However, this trend does Bely the fact that the relationship and balance of power has changed.

This also means companies need to get creative in making sure they have multiple talent supply chain sources to get the talent they need to survive and thrive. It is no longer enough to focus on traditional models of workforce and recruitment. Maybe it's about looking at the roles, skills and output needed collectively and deciding what talent model makes the most sense. It's about looking at talent more holistically and deciding on when and where you need permanent talent ("the core") that drive the company forward, maintain the culture, build and drive long term strategy. Then looking at the ecosystem of other talent; independent consultants, crowd sourcing, contract labor, that provide unique skills, on-demand support, can align with fluctuating or seasonal demand, provide niche skills to support a company's growth and strategy. It's not that employees are "more important" or have "higher skills"; it's that every worker contributes their unique skills, talent, personality for the greater good of the whole, the organization. This works for both sides; the people who want the flexibility and freedom to work independently, or those who want to be an employee for a number of reasons, and the corporations that employ them. Everyone is on more equal ground. Permanent employees have less of a chance of being let go of even though there is another population of workforce that is flexible and can accommodate peaks and valleys in market demand, financial changes, and so on. The key is those in the flexible workforce are choosing to be there. Ultimately, it's about embracing this new model of work and looking at how to accommodate and respect this workforce under a new model that has not had an update since the industrial revolution.

So what does THAT look like? This new model of workforce is made up of permanent employees, contractors, independent consultants, returning retirees, part time working mothers (I threw that in, one can dream), freelancers, cloud sourcing. There is so much talk about workers' rights and protections; that is, benefits for independent consultants and contractors who contribute side by side with your employees.

"Every day, tens of thousands of people stream into Google offices wearing red name badges. They eat in Google's cafeterias, ride its commuter shuttles and work alongside its celebrated geeks. But they can't access all of the company's celebrated perks. They aren't entitled to stock and can't enter certain offices. Many don't have health insurance." Per Inside Google's Invisible Workforce Aug. 2018.

The article goes on to say, *"Those contractors outnumbered direct employees for the first time in the company's twenty-year history. Another issue Google employees are discussing bringing to management is the state of the contract workforce, according to four people familiar with the conversations. Yana Calou, an organizer with advocacy group Coworker.org who speaks with Google employees and contractors, said that both groups are concerned about the workers who aren't full Google employees. 'They feel isolated, precarious and like second-class citizens,' Calou said. 'It's a microcosm of what's happening in the economy as a whole.'"*

I'd like to offer another perspective. There are trade-offs to working as in independent consultant or contractor. You get higher pay (usually), flexibility (and yes some instability as a result) and don't "have any of the political hassles and drama " – said my friend Meredith who used to be a corporate executive but now has the same role at the same company as a consultant and is much happier. With that freedom and flexibility, you pass up on some of the "perks" of an employee. Some call these perks "hand cuffs" but that convo is for another day.

Apparently, this workforce takes on these opportunities with eyes wide open. There is a tradeoff for the flexibility and freedom that come with working this way. However, there is definitely work to do in ensuring this workforce feels appreciated, validated and respected, regardless of the fact of whether they are an employee or a non-employee. That is universal for every human and it is extremely important.

Benefits and equal pay have been around since World War II as a direct result of wage controls imposed by the federal government during World War II. The labor market was tight because of the increased demand for goods and decreased supply of workers during the war. Federally imposed wage and price controls prohibited manufacturers and other employers from raising wages enough to attract workers. When the War Labor Board declared that fringe benefits, such as sick leave and health insurance, did not count as wages for the purpose of wage controls, employers responded with significantly increased offers of fringe benefits, especially health care coverage, to attract workers. Health benefits were not created to "protect" workers, but an incentive to attract more workers. Today, maybe those incentives are now being eclipsed by other incentives that draw talent, like freedom and flexibility. This is a question that calls for consideration.

Today, independent consultants can purchase their own healthcare and build it into their bill rates. Contractors can participate in staffing provider benefits due to the ACA requirements to provide benefits if you have a workforce bigger than fifty. As the traditional "employee" model erodes to fit a new landscape where technology, global mobility and social changes are happening, the "protections" provided seem a bit outdated. What protections does a worker need? I know independent consultants who have their pick of clients to work for. The key to their safety and stability is the marketability of their skill set and experience.

I was reading a quote yesterday; from a Forbes article "The Next Hot Market – Freelancers". Carl Camden, the ex CEO of Kelly Services, one of the world's largest staffing providers, who now founded IPSE U.S. – The Association of Independent Workers, an advocacy group for Independent Workers. He goes on to say "There is a group of people who desperately want to be employees," Camden says. "To a large degree, the reason they want this is our country has put in so many barriers to pursuing independent work. The only way to get access to the safety net easily in our country is as an employee."

His heart is in the right place changes are needed, but he's missing the point. This workforce is this workforce precisely because they do NOT want to be an employee. Let's go back to the Uber Drivers I talk about on a daily basis as I shoot around to client appointments. Few if any talk about desperately wanting to be an employee, some of them already are and this is their side gig. However, Carl does point out there is room for the regulatory bodies and IRS to catch up with this new workforce landscape and provide tax breaks and healthcare discounts that many large corporations enjoy. These workers don't need "protection." Their marketability and skill set is their protection to ensure continued work. But they do need to be recognized.

"A sense of security keeps many "handcuffed" to working in corporations. However the rise of the gig economy is changing the rule. Values matter and people will leave if they aren't aligned personally." Says Carolyn Swora, founder of Pinnacle Culture and HR Talent and Strategy Consulting Company.

We are at an inflection point, where outdated regulatory requirements and labor laws no longer fit the new normal workforce landscape. This new breed of worker is contributing at an equal level to society, the gross national product, and corporate growth as a traditional employee. They need access to affordable healthcare, sustainable tax thresholds, fair and timely payments. But what does that support look like? The "protections" typically provided by corporations are not leaving employees feeling all that "protected" as the Great Recession proved. Maybe these workers don't need to be "protected." Maybe they need to be valued, respected, paid on time, given access to affordable healthcare, and leave the rest up to the market. Maybe it's the construct of those "protections" that made them seek out independent employment in the first place.

"This week; New York became the first major American city to halt new vehicle licenses for ride-hail services, dealing a significant setback to Uber in its largest market in the United States. The legislation passed by the City Council will cap the number of for-hire vehicles for a year while the city studies the booming industry. The bill also allows New York to set a minimum pay rate for drivers." Uber Hit with Cap as New York City Takes Lead in Crackdown – New York times 8/8/18

The article goes on to state more than one hundred thousand workers and their families will see an immediate benefit from this legislation. Mayor de Blasio said while referring to the city's army of for-hire drivers, "And this action will stop the influx of cars contributing to the congestion grinding our streets to a halt." Many taxi and Uber drivers say they support the cap proposal. They hope it will halt the flood of new vehicles clogging city streets and allow them to make more trips and improve their earnings. ***Uber and other ride-hail services could add new vehicles only if they are wheelchair accessible.***

The proposed plan is to provide a minimum wage within which if a driver's earnings fall below seventeen dollars and twenty-two cents ($17.22) per hour over the course of a week, the companies (Uber/Lyft) would be required to make up the difference. A study by the Taxi and Limousine Commission suggested the companies could absorb this cost partly by lowering their commissions, which range from about ten to twenty-five percent of passenger fares on average. The median net hourly earnings in the industry were about fourteen dollar and twenty-five cents ($14.25), the study found.

It is uncertain how the minimum wage will be enforced and how will that impact the market? Is a "minimum wage" even necessary or relevant in the gig economy? Will it artificially inflate or deflate the market and opportunities? Is a minimum wage relevant today in an economy where you can modulate the hours, times and how you work? I would be curious how the study was conducted and how the hours/wages were calculated? An Uber drivers' time is spent very differently in an hour than a traditional worker spends their time.

The reality is, change is happening, and in some cases violently. We must put in the work to address this new normal in the way we work. Applying outdated models, such as minimum wage, benefits, and so on that were set in motion to address a workforce landscape that no longer exists is a limited approach. But you have to start somewhere.

My friend, collaborator and one time client; Sean Ring, co-founder of Fulcrum, A talent cloud solution believes that traditional employment is eroding permanently and morphing into something else entirely. Something more fluid; for the employer and the employee. He believes further that the traditional relationship between employer and employee is null and void. 'We need to refresh the archaic employment construct," says Sean. Maybe the employment construct is changing with or without us.

Maybe it's about an equitable exchange of services and support for compensation. A co-collaboration rather than a patriarchal employer – employee relationship where the balance of power is with the employer; the one who can hire and fire at will.

If that is the case, what does that new construct look like? What does it look like today and even ten years from now? Many industry experts and economists say the workforce landscape will change dramatically in the next five to ten years. It will be a mixture of AI, traditional and nontraditional workers, with melting geographical boundaries as more work is done off site and remotely, and work is based on outcomes and intellectual property. This will be more so as we move towards embracing what workers can deliver from a service based economy and moving away from a manufacturing based economy. And who are the various workers that make up the non-traditional workforce which we are lumping into one category; the Gig Workforce? One of the biggest challenges we hear from clients is the confusion over terms; gig worker, contractors, independent consultant, talent cloud, crowd sourced, freelancers. What is the difference? What do they want? Why are there so many of them? How did they come to dominate our workforce market, and why? In the next chapter we will cover what the gig workforce is, what was the genesis of their growth, and how they fit into the traditional workforce models.

Chapter 4: What is the Gig Workforce?

There is so much confusion! Over the terminology. The new wave of change in the workplace presents us with terms such as shared economy, gig worker, freelancer, independent consultant, contractor, and so on. Who are these workers, what is the difference between the terms and why are there so many and growing?

The definitions are not necessarily tied to the skills or role of the worker, but rather the way they are engaged. Here are some basic definitions below to get that out of the way. These definitions are as provided by "The Gig Economy and Alternative Work Arrangements" – Gallup 2018

Worker Type	Definition	Example
CONTRACT FIRM WORKERS	Employees who work for a company that provides their services to another entity on a contractual or project basis	A traveling nurse who is hired and placed by a staffing firm in a hospital for a three-month rotation during a nursing shortage
INDEPENDENT CONTRACTORS	People who provide goods and services under a specific contractual agreement to another entity	A freelance graphic design consultant who is self-employed and redesigns logos and advertisements for small to mid-sized businesses
ON-CALL WORKERS	Those who only work on an as-needed basis, not including workers who work on-call shifts as part of their regular job	A substitute teacher who works for several different school districts and only works when there is an open teaching vacancy
ONLINE PLATFORM WORKERS	Workers who find short jobs through a mobile or online marketplace that connects them directly with customers, either in person or online	A delivery driver who picks up dry cleaning, grocery or food items and delivers the product directly to the customer via a mobile platform request
TEMPORARY WORKERS	Workers who have short-term work arrangements, often assigned to them by a temporary or staffing agency	A data entry specialist who is given a short-term assignment entering medical records into a system for a healthcare organization

Gig workers are all workers who have any of the above alternative work arrangement as their primary job.

These definitions have come about in recent years. But gig workers are not a new concept.

As so often happens in fashion and economics, what was old is new again. Gigging is a way of life that is not all that different from the way we lived prior to the industrial revolution.

Per Tawny Paul, a British historian, "While it might seem that long-established ways of working are being disrupted, history shows us that one-person, one career model is a relatively recent phenomenon.

Prior to industrialization in the nineteenth century, most people worked multiple jobs to piece together a living. Looking to the past uncovers some of the challenges, benefits and consequences of a gig economy." Paul said.

The early eighteenth century gig worker might look something like this; by day, you could be a barber, renting a small shop, shaving customer's heads, crafting wigs. In the off hours you could work as a book dealer and eventually an auctioneer, selling various items in alehouses. All of this, done without the delivery system of technology available today that brings together buyer and seller in automating transactions.

What is the makeup of the gig worker, why are they growing so quickly? We spoke earlier about freedom, flexibility and pursuing your passion. What about the more "reluctant" gig workers, who are filling in time and getting some cash flow till they find permanent work? This is the workforce so many politicians and other advocates are saying are being disenfranchised. They can't feed their families or make ends meet. It is hard to determine how much of this workforce is there by choice or reluctantly. However, as at September 2018, the unemployment rate is at a fifty year low of thirty-seven percent. Despite the availability of permanent jobs, the gig workforce continues to grow. Why? Are workers choosing this path over traditional work arrangements? Is it because of AI and the speed of technology eliminating jobs that belonged to the service sector? Is it because that is the only work they can get in lieu of a permanent job because their skill set is not at the level for higher paying jobs? Do these workers have the opportunities to up level their skill sets to make a higher wage? I think there is more work to be done here but we also live in a capitalist society. You are compensated for your skill set and value in the marketplace. That is and always will be at the core of the American Dream.

Maybe it's Darwinism again at work. Survival of the fittest. We as a species are being forced out of lower wage, lower skilled, repetitive task jobs to leverage the higher skills that separate us from the robots. Maybe we are taking the reins and changing the employer/employee relationship. We have our hands on the wheel (aka best quote ever from "Hustle and Flow" if you ever watched the movie) and we are deciding how, when, and why we work. The different terms and definitions that have cropped up to define this workforce point to the fact that this is going beyond a passing trend.

To give you an idea of its importance, as of today, the gig workforce is contributing seven hundred and fifteen billion dollars to the economy. Who is this gig worker? What is the personality and profile of your typical gig worker?

That's what is so interesting. There is no "typical" profile of the gig worker. It's the teacher driving Uber during the summer to supplement his income, the retiree who decides to go back to work part time as a consultant; it's the technology developer in Argentina who you'll find on an on-demand gig workforce platform like Toptal providing support for a Pitney Bowes manager in Colorado. It's the stay at home new mother who is highly educated and wants to work part time; you can find her on the Mom Project, and on-demand workforce website that brokers projects for stay at home mothers and encourages more gender diversity. It's basically every gender, every skill set and background, every race, economic class, age, and it knows no geographic boundaries, thanks to digital technology. They all do however have one thing in common. They have traded stability and a steady paycheck for flexibility and control, some willingly and some reluctantly.

There is a shift happening; employees are disenchanted with the corporate lifestyle which includes long and stressful days, poor work/life balance and salaries not keeping pace with inflation. Some of those reluctant gig workers may be taking another view of going back to a full time job. And some may not. It's not for everyone. You have to be okay with inconsistent pay, constantly changing roles and deliverables, demanding and unreasonable clients, and most importantly the buck starts with YOU. There is no one else to blame if things go wrong. When you work for someone else, there is always someone else to blame. As a friend once said "The bigger the company, the more places for mediocrity to hide." Not so as a gig worker.

Something is happening in labor and job growth that confirms the rise of the gig workforce is not a passing fad. "We find that 94% of net job growth in the past decade was in the alternative work category," said Alan Krueger famous labor economist. "And over 60% was due to the [the rise] of independent contractors, freelancers and contract company workers." In other words, nearly all of the ten million jobs created. Critics counter that this trend could signal the deterioration of the social contract between employees and employers, as some organizations employ more contingent workers to cut liabilities and costs, such as taxes and employee benefits. Seems like the social contract has deteriorated on its own and maybe that needed to happen?

There is a perception that gig or non-traditional workers will be less "loyal" or productive. That couldn't be further from the truth. Per Gallup's "The Gig Economy and Alternative Work Arrangements" paper, Gig Workers are MORE loyal and productive. Gig economy workers with more independent roles — independent contractors (39%) and online platform workers (36%) — are more engaged than traditional workers (27%). Maybe to go back to my friends quote; there is no room for mediocrity to hide when your employment is performance dependent.

We do need to recognize this workforce. They are here, they are contributing, and the government and advocacy groups are looking at the gig workforce as its own labor category that is here and growing. They are asking and trying to figure out how to count this workforce. They keep questioning, "How do we make sure they are taken care of?"

Or maybe big business no longer has to "take care of" this workforce? The reason many are choosing to work this way is because now they are not interested in the golden handcuffs of a stable job and steady paycheck. Maybe the price to pay is too high. Some of those workers who wore the handcuffs for decades are stepping up to the gig workforce plate as well. Maybe we need to change the definition of "taking care of" this workforce. The motivators for the new workforce landscape have changed.

Interestingly enough; according to research from MBO Partners, people age fifty-three and older made up thirty-five percent of those doing independent or gig work in 2017, up from thirty-three percent in 2016. They like the flexibility and because they are valued for their expertise and experience. This is a group that came up during the boom years for job growth and healthy economy, when the standard was to go to college and get a high paying job. They tasted the best corporate America has to give and yet, they are the fastest growing population in the Gig Economy. Maybe because they are seeing the value of what they bring to the table and want to make a living on their own terms.

I get the appeal of the steady job, don't get me wrong. I left a two hundred thousand dollar a year job and the first three years of building my consultancy practice was tough. I was broke, stressed, lonely and working eighteen hours a week and dealing with mind bending doubt and fear on a daily basis. I sold everything to keep going; my house, car, furniture, cashed in my 401K and pension, and one year had over three thousand dollars in NSF charges from my bank. On top of all this, I was told by many "experts" that my trademarked model and approach was "spot on but too early 'for anyone to buy into it. In addition to this, I was dealing with the fact that I was probably completely insane and my business idea was not viable.

At my lowest point, I remember I had to borrow one thousand dollars from my father to keep going. It was heartbreaking, he is retired and funds are tight for him. He suggested maybe I want to consider going back to work as an executive. I could see where he was coming from. It was logical. The daughter who was always able to pick up the tab and give everyone expensive gifts was having to borrow one thousand to keep from being evicted. So why didn't I just give up and go back? Because I couldn't, because I tasted freedom and I was hooked. I was hooked on creating my own path, making money on my terms and using all my creative and intellectual gifts to create a viable and thriving company. Money was tight and signs of success were few...but I was hooked, yeah maybe even obsessed. The thought of going back to a regular corporate executive job was horrifying. It would be more than just giving up and accepting I failed. I could handle that embarrassment. It was the thought of having to go back and work for someone else, see someone else get the credit for my ideas, build their dream, watch them get the fruits of my labor, all for the promise of a steady paycheck and decent benefits. Well somewhat steady, all of us have been fired at least once right? I had shape shifted into someone who could never fit in that environment again. I knew this on a cellular level. I also promised my family I would succeed. They motivate me every day.

So maybe there is also something deeper going on, there is a specific makeup and psychology of the gig worker? Maybe it's more than just social and behavioral changes, or the demise of the traditional employment construct. Maybe we are seeing a new breed of human and workforce emerging? That slightly mad, creative, independent human that for the first time in two hundred years sees the potential in these shifts happening, and the technology and AI making it possible to work this way to make a living. This person now has a viable way to channel those gifts and make a living and life and go beyond that to be the top three percent in success and income. Or at least make a steady enough income to live comfortably.

With the availability of social media and technology (aka free marketing), we have opportunities today that have never existed until now to make a living, create a brand, and create a company. My friend's son is 14 years old. He sells homemade slime and his Instagram channel has over 1M followers. He makes over seventy thousand dollars a year in sales and sponsors. I don't think I hit that income level till my late 30's. There are senior citizens working remotely as interpreters, editors, customer service reps, all from the comfort of their home via on-demand talent cloud platforms. This option did not exist ten years ago. You can ask any senior citizen. It beats wearing the orange blazers at home depot any day. They get to use their greatest gifts; intellectual property, years of experience in a specialized field and there is a dignity and respect in that kind of work. With everyone living longer, and outliving decimated 401k's and social security on its last legs; providing a way to make a living, that uses your greatest gifts, allows you to work how, when and where you want to, seems like a good thing. The gig economy is very human friendly that way, despite the concerns about lack of social safety nets, and AI, and unpredictable pay. Maybe these "issues" will someday be redefined as part and parcel of working this way and the benefits far outweigh the concerns.

This gig workface is a catalyst for new laws, and we've just started to really take this category seriously. Like any kind of revolutionary change; first comes the explosive event, resistance, adaptation, and then acceptance. Okay, this is not an official trajectory by some famous social scientist, I made it up on the fly but I think it fits. Feel free to use at your leisure.

As I write this book, we are on the cusp of a major change; more and more articles are cropping up about the gig economy, with questions such as "is it good, is it bad, is it destroying work as we know it?" Those leaders that are at the forefront, gig technology platforms and talent cloud providers share statistics about the growth of this workforce, the pay scales, the freedom and flexibility; how it's changing the way we work for the better. Independent consultants are contributing blogs and articles about how to maximize the gig economy, for profit and a sustainable, comfortable living. Some have "how to" blog posts or published books on how to market and brand yourself as an independent consultant. However with this dearth of information, thought leaders, professional organizations dedicated to the gig economy, many organizations and HR and Talent leaders still seem very much in the dark and more confused than ever on how, when, why and if they should leverage this new worker. And solution providers are coming to their aid to sort out the confusion and mitigate some of the fears or provide a viable solution. Per Connie Wendt, V.P. of Compliance and Relations at ClearPath, a company that provides an overview of the issues surrounding worker classification and a review of organization's worker potential risk and exposure for Independent Contractor compliance. "I'm often taken aback by the responses we get. Everything from... our finance, legal, vendor management, etc. department handles that we have a process for IC's, we don't need any help there, or we handle government contracts so I'm sure our compliance is up-to-speed." Organizations are still struggling to come to grips with this new workforce and where they fit in.

Many organizations are still working with outdated views of using the gig workforce as part of their total workforce strategy. Ten years ago, most organizations used independent consultants and contractors sparingly, and as fill in for someone out on medical leave, or to accommodate fluctuations in demand. Today, this workforce is just as important as your permanent workforce, and with technology providing the delivery system, it is easier than ever to source and onboard this talent. But is that all it takes? The answer to that question is "sort of." The immediate availability and access to this talent, due to technology is creating as many questions as answers. Organizations today are not sure where this workforce fits in. How do they treat them, train them, do they need to train them?

Companies are now just beginning to look at how to treat their gig workforce; they are not employees, don't get employee benefits, or other perks. Yet they are now working side by side with other employees, and are just as important to the success of an organization. Do they need to be treated the same as employees? Is that the question?

Or is it about looking at the individual and ensuring they feel respected, appreciated, inspired to work for you and your company regardless of their classification? Are the lines becoming blurred? Maybe they should be...maybe there shouldn't be any lines. Each of these types of workers needs different things. An independent consultant working as a software engineer in Argentina is not going to need the same level of oversight and support as the employee down the hall from the manager's office, working on a team. What about the temporary contractor there for six months who is working on site? Where do they fit in within the normal construct of training, retention, and management?

As the fluid workforce becomes more the norm; company leaders and middle managers' jobs become much more complex with regards to oversight, management, and training of its teams and workforce. Or does it? As more work is done via networks and teams versus following a top-down management approach, is that easier or harder to manage? When was the last time you had a company meeting in an office? How many of them are now done via Skype, Uber conference, to pull together all the players on a project, initiative or team? Maybe not everyone "needs" to be "managed". Maybe the leaders of today need to look across their teams and networks of employees, contractors, independent consultants, talent cloud and figure out how to best inspire and support this workforce, on their terms, to ensure the best outcomes. Maybe it's a "human" approach, the golden rule of workforce management, across all categories.

Maybe the next biggest change in the way we work is looking at traditional management protocol and "employee" retention and training models. Maybe that is the next major shift in our new normal workforce landscape. How do corporate leaders accommodate and integrate this new workforce within their companies to ensure the best outcomes for both sides of the equation? The rise of the Gig workforce is forcing companies to rethink everything about their talent strategy and how work gets done.

Chapter 5: Why The Gig Workforce Is Flipping The Script On How And Why We Work

"No economy can succeed without a high-quality workforce, particularly in an age of globalization and technical change." ~ Ben Bernanke

The definitions of when and where you find "high quality" workforce is changing. How work is performed and the way we work has radically changed. Many say we are moving to a flexible organizational structure; now it's about co-creating rather than managing. It's about networks and teams rather than top down management.

Thirty years ago this framework for working would not make sense. It was about permanent employees, working 9:00-5:00, in office buildings, with very specific roles and reporting hierarchy. It was birthday cake celebrations in the conference room, and conversations by the water cooler. The guy (or girl, but mostly guys) at the top, with directors and managers below, and supporting staff, all working towards specific directives. There were specific mission statements and annual performance reviews everyone agreed to. Working from home was a "luxury" and you had to drag home a behemoth docking station and heavy laptop (the height of sophisticated technology). If you used a consultant or contractor, it was to fill in for someone sick, or for a short term project. You set up a contract with a big 5 consulting firm or staffing provider and you paid them from your procurement system after receiving an invoice.

The thought of outsourcing a specific project to remote teams, or using technology to deliver a fully vetted independent contractor to your front desk (or do the work from Russia) was unheard of and would certainly not be viewed as smart way to get work done. Would they be reliable? Can someone really stay focused on their work if they are working from home or not standing around the water cooler and putting in "face time?"

Times have changed. We have ways of getting work done that are unprecedented. We have income streams that did not exist before; we can share our home or our RV, jump in our car, and spend a few hours "juicing" up scooters, doing odd jobs, setting up a side hustle via on-demand platforms. The way we make money and a living has radically changed.

We are choosing to work differently, and offer our services, skills and experience on terms that better fit the way we want to live, work and contribute to the world in the few years we have on this planet. We are changing the game around how work is getting done, and the employers and businesses; big and small are scrambling to adapt.

But what came first? The growth in the gig economy changed the way organizations get work done, or did it come from big enterprise organizations who want to "save money" and "not pay benefits" and the "devaluating of the worker"? Today I saw the first AI news anchor debuted from China. China's state-run news agency just unveiled the AI-powered anchor at China's World Internet Conference. The news anchor is modeled on a real presenter named Zhang Zhow. The anchor learns from live broadcast videos and is able to man the news desk 24-hours a day. He is snappily dressed and looks like a programmer I knew several years back.

The reality is, perhaps, it's not the gig workers OR the Enterprise organizations driving this change. Maybe it's a confluence of different social, economic, behavioral, technology changes happening all at once that is changing the landscape.

The growth of the gig economy is part of our natural evolution. Not only are we choosing to work differently, and on our terms, but the world is changing. Technology is making it possible for global teams to collaborate across time zones via zoom meeting and Skype to get work done. A modern day team today could be a project manager in New York City managing a team of developers in Argentina and Russia, with his direct reports in Ohio or Atlanta, all collaborating over email, Slack chat, etc. to complete a project.

The gig workforce is growing and it is forcing enterprise organizations to think differently about how work gets done. And it's just a small part of a bigger change; this is being coined now as the "Fourth Industrial Revolution." Per Wikipedia; it is the fourth major industrial era since the initial Industrial Revolution of the 18th century. It is characterized by a fusion of technologies that is blurring the lines between the physical, digital, and biological spheres, collectively referred to as cyber-physical systems. It is marked by emerging technology breakthroughs in a number of fields, including robotics, artificial intelligence, nanotechnology, quantum computing, biotechnology, the Internet of Things, the Industrial Internet of Things (IOT), fifth-generation wireless technologies (5G), additive manufacturing/3D printing and fully autonomous vehicles.

So the humans are not only changing the way work gets done, but there is a technology evolution as well. Technology is replacing the mundane, repetitive, processing work that was so much a part of the first industrial revolution. This perfect storm of technology, AI, access across geographies and time zones; a blurring of the lines across time zones, countries, is leveraging the best the "humans" have to offer. It's enabling access to the best and brightest talent in ways that did not exist even ten years ago, much less one hundred years ago.

This new industrial revolution is providing new ways of getting work done and connecting talent in unprecedented ways. We need to radically change the way work gets done; and how and with whom and what that work gets done. We need to do this today to accommodate how people want to work today.

It's not just about making a hiring decision anymore. When we think about growth for a company or expanding our workforce, the go to of hiring an employee and beginning the process has radically changed. We need to think about it differently; do we hire an employee? Or can we bring on an independent consultant? Can we crowd source this work, or do we need a person at all? The availability of different models around how work gets done is both a blessing and a curse. Many of our clients are faced with these challenges and are not sure how to build new talent acquisition and workforce strategies around these choices. The explosion in the gig workforce and the supporting technology and services that enable sourcing, delivery, on boarding, paying, is providing choices and options that did not exist before in how work gets done. It's also creating more questions than answers? How do we train this workforce? Or do we need to? How do we manage them, ensure they are engaged and feel like a part of the team? Or maybe we don't need to worry about making them feel like they are part of the team? Maybe those modes of managing and engaging your workforce are outdated too. Everyone wants to feel respected and appreciated, but maybe we need to change the model around what that looks like depending on the workforce you are engaging?

I saw an article today in Fast Company Magazine; "Should you Include Freelancers in your Talent Development Program?" As freelancers take on new responsibilities in your organization, it may be time to consider investing in them, says Mike Boro, a partner in PwC's Workforce of the Future practice. "I do think there is a war for talent, there is a war for independent contractors, so the better you can do to get your independent contractors integrated and then learning something which advances their skill set is actually a positive as well," he says.

The lines are becoming blurred as more and more gig workers become a part of a company's workforce. We need to look at them differently; they are not just a temporary fill in, or providing a niche skill set for a short period of time (although this is also true), but they are now the foundation of our workforce and are making significant contributions to a company's bottom line, growth and product.

They are offering a fresh perspective, bringing innovation, global experience, and they want to contribute and create. They are changing the whole makeup of the workforce in general. They won't be staying long in most cases, less than a year, but what they create, contribute, and change will be a part of a company's legacy. So how do companies change to accommodate short term talent and assignments? How can we structure work, projects, and deliverables to adapt to this fluid workforce? Or maybe this will happen organically as the fourth industrial revolution takes hold, and we are forced to look at how work gets done and change the rules radically. The byproduct of changing the way work gets done and embracing this new normal makes for a happier, more productive workforce perhaps? People get to work on projects that excite them; they get the flexibility and freedom that contributes to higher satisfaction rates. As companies look at how to get work done in exciting new ways, the "human factor" is also undergoing big changes in the fourth industrial revolution. Many say that the erosion of the traditional employer/employee construct is a bad thing; maybe it's not good or bad, but just a natural evolution of man (and women) and machine co-existing.

Prior to this construct, it was factories, machines, production lines and organizational design coexisting.

Today it's technology, AI, Machine learning, coexisting with (or replacing) the humans to get work done.

Given that we have changed, and the millennials are influencing the workforce today, this new industrial revolution is a reflection back to us of where we are, how we want to live, how we want to be treated and respected in the workplace, how we want to produce, and earn a living. We don't want to give our lives away to a company for forty years, and do work that doesn't matter to us, within a rigid schedule and sit in a gray cubicle.

So where do employers; enterprise organizations fit into all of this? Do they have a say? Are they even participating or driving this explosion in the gig workforce or are they reacting to it? Employers are trying to figure out how to change their traditional workforce models to fit this new normal. I believe both sides of the equation are benefitting from this more fluid workforce and the behaviors of traditional corporate America have created some backlash that has contributed to the explosive growth in the gig workforce. But back to Darwin again; survival of the fittest, ecosystems change and adapt. So in a way, there is something very organic and natural about what has happened to the way we work.

Both "organisms" have changed. Corporate America is no longer promising stability and longevity because it knows it can't. Market conditions shift too rapidly; the lifespan of a company is shortening. Jeff Bezos said it best in a recent interview overheard by CNBC.

"Amazon is not too big to fail," Bezos said, "In fact, I predict one day Amazon will fail. Amazon will go bankrupt. If you look at large companies, their life spans tend to be thirty-plus years, not a hundred-plus years." Jeff goes on to say "The key to prolonging that demise, is for the company to "obsess over customers" and to avoid looking inward, worrying about itself."

"The average age of a company listed on the S&P 500 has fallen from almost 60 years old in the 1950s to less than 20 years currently," a team of Credit Suisse analysts led by Eugene Klerk wrote in a note to investors Thursday. **"Technology killing off corporate America: Average life span of companies under 20 years - CNBC**

The article goes on to say; "The disruptive force of technology is killing off older companies earlier and at a much faster rate than decades ago, squeezing employees, investors and other stakeholders, according to a new report." Automation is the No. 1 "disruptive force."

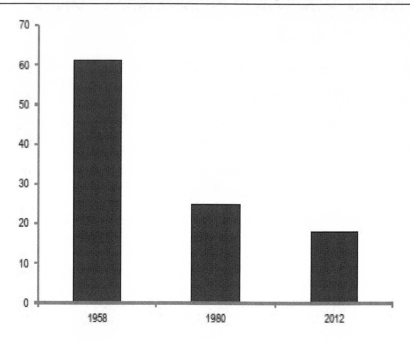

So company's life spans are shortening in perfect harmony to the shifting models for how work gets done. Is this a coincidence, or just the natural order of things? Today, millennials and gen Z don't want to work for a company for thirty years. They want fulfillment, flexibility, excitement, and the chance to make a difference. This works out because companies will not be around long enough for them to collect the gold watch and pension. Again Darwinism at its finest. Both sides of the equation are adapting and reacting to the other, and changing as a result to conform to the new order.

So maybe the Gig Workforce is not changing the way we work after all; maybe it's just a natural evolution of the new order of things. Brought about by specific catalysts; the Great Recession, Technology explosion, AI and Machine Learning, changes in how we want to spend our time and how we want to work, constantly shifting market demand and trends, generational trends. There is a certain synergy in all these different trends coming together at just this moment? Perhaps. This isn't scientific. I am sure a well educated economist or other scholarly person reading this (thank you by the way) will dispute my less than scientific statement. But it can't all be coincidence?

Maybe the explosive growth in the gig economy is not a catalyst or driver at all. Maybe it's a natural new order, evolving because of all the other shifts occurring. Or as my friend Don Jackson always says "It's a Mind Shift." (He uses this example frequently for just about everything that can't be easily explained.) The unemployment rate continues to go down, and yet workers are continuing to work independently. Big Consulting Firms like McKinssey and Deloitte are coming out with new norms for the "Future of Work." "Intrapreneurship" will be more prevalent within organizations. They state that global distribution of the workforce will be the norm, with smaller teams working together. "Want" vs. "Need" will prevail in workers' attitudes towards their career; they will choose alternatives to traditional employment; places they WANT to work, not necessarily NEED to work. With more intrapreneurship and collaboration trumping traditional hierarchy models, information will not just "flow down" but flow bottom up and side to side. Bureaucracy and red tape will take a back seat to this new normal. This shift will also move companies to focus on prosperity over profit with a focus on worker health and wellness and making a positive impact on the world. Collaborative technology will be the "connectivity glue" to hold it all together for organizations' operations. These are radical changes in how we conduct business and work today.

This shift is changing the way that whole organizations look at their models, practices/processes, culture and infrastructure. The business environment has shifted; rapidly changing global markets, hyper-competition, digitations, advanced technology and talent/skill insufficiencies. This makes workforce agility all that much more important. It's a key enabler for organizational agility.

For organizations to achieve this agility, it goes beyond sourcing and managing external and internal workforce in new ways. In a way, workforce agility must carry the whole concrete organization on its back; that is, the benefits of workforce agility (versus mere staff aug and permanent workers) are gated by the state of the organization and all that it consists contains.

Data indicate that most organizations do not have sufficiently developed capabilities to achieve workforce and, more importantly, organizational agility — despite the fact that doing so will be necessary to succeed, if not survive, in the coming years. It is therefore necessary for executives to be realistic and appreciate the magnitude and scope of the challenge and embracing, understanding and implementing a talent and workforce strategy.

The intraprenurial spirit that is the foundation of the gig economy can yield many benefits for organizations. Despite what many say about lack of "commitment" and "adhering to company culture," that is often the perception of those not familiar with utilizing nontraditional labor. Data already points to higher satisfaction and higher commitment rates of independent and contract workers over permanent talent. Anytime you have a happier, more satisfied workforce, you have a company that is prosperous and positioned for growth. This workforce thinks differently about work. They bring a level of innovation, focus and commitment that can infuse a corporate culture with new energy and excitement. As we talked about earlier, because of the "unstable" nature of independent work, there is even more focus on performing and contributing. As a gig worker, your income depends on it.

The workforce itself is also adjusting to this new normal. Many participating in the gig economy are still holding on to more traditional norms in the employment construct; benefits, stable pay, other corporate perks, while embracing the flexibility and freedom that makes this so attractive. Workers and Organizations are still struggling with navigating the new relationship and what that looks like.

Co-employment lawsuits are still happening to companies like Uber and Google, but more companies are also pushing back and winning. The tide is turning. Regulators, politicians and Bureau of Labor are coming to a sort of reckoning about the "ten factor test" and CA's Supreme Court Ruling on the "ABC" Test (issued April' 2018) (listed below) which both define who a worker is;

(A) The worker is *free from control* and direction of the hiring entity in connection with the performance of the work, both under the contract for performance of the work and in fact;

(B) The worker performs work that is *outside the course of the hiring entity's business*; and

(C) The worker is customarily engaged in an independently established trade, occupation, or business.

These qualifiers and tests are not practical or relevant in this new normal. Many large companies have come out against it, stating that it will stifle creativity and innovation. It is also damaging industry that rely heavily on using independent consultants as a normal part of doing business where both sides benefit and enjoy this construct. Such businesses include tattoo parlors, yoga instructors and so on. So far, it works for both sides.

I foresee in less than five years, these laws will shift again; to something more flexible and less punitive to allow for the growth and integration of this workforce into every organization.

Yes, we need to look at the social safety nets, and revaluate how we want to accommodate, count, regulate, and enable this workforce. In fact, as we stated earlier in this book, this is already happening; with portable benefits and insurance packages targeted to independent workers. Every facet of traditional work is being tested and broken and rebuilt into something else.

The "staples" or some might call it "golden handcuffs" of traditional employment like health benefits, steady paycheck, company perks are being replicated by other service providers and tech companies to support the non-traditional workforce, as stated earlier in this book. Companies providing insurance, portable benefits; companies like Qwil providing instant pay (for a small fee) so enterprising independent workers can get their money right away instead of waiting forty-five days. They are getting big wads of VC capital and attention from larger companies like Microsoft and ADP because they see these companies as viable and enablers of the more agile workforce. These companies are becoming the new social construct for this new breed of worker. The gig economy is not destroying the social construct; it's reinventing it.

This shift in how social safety nets are being viewed is very recent. Over the past couple of years, these tech startups and service providers have assumed the position of providing a new social safety net and this is very new. The concept is new. So workers and employers alike are still struggling to navigate through the maze of choices. It's the reason why companies like Google who utilize more independent workers than they do permanent employees are becoming front and center of this controversy around protections and rights for these workers. The regulatory bodies and laws that are used as the benchmark to determine if leveraging this workforce is violating laws or providing potential risk of co-employment lawsuits were established starting twenty years ago and were set up in a way that severely limited the use of non-traditional labor in favor of using a more traditional workforce. Well what do you do if most workers no longer want to work in a traditional way?

What does that look like? What if everything you knew about how to build a workforce, how long they will work, where they come from, what incentivizes them, has completely changed? How do you adapt and change your recruiting strategy? Given a company is only as good as its best talent (and market share) how does a company look at its Talent Strategy now?

We are on a precipice of a new frontier. The way, how, and why people work has completely changed. And we are revolutionizing a model of how work gets done that has been in place for over two hundred years, where the employer has had the upper hand. A person needs "a job"; they send in a resume to HR "The Boss" who hopefully see's their amazing credentials and hires them for a decent salary and good benefits. That model has shifted radically. The "employer" no longer has the upper hand and they are struggling to catch up with the changes. Through no fault of their own; they are navigating many changes in technology, workforce shifts, dynamic markets and digital media and hyper connectivity where information is disseminated immediately. Today, prospective employees have a flood of information on your company; Glassdoor, Google, Reuters. They can look up salaries you are already paying, all the roles you have available on Indeed, and have many choices for earning a living you offer. The choices available today are typically not all as a traditional permanent employee.

The side of the worker has shifted much more rapidly, and agility, flexibly and freedom are key. They are aware of the choices available, can leverage multiple channels to earn a living; such as combining a permanent job plus a side hustle, working independently from where they are; and their office could be a Starbucks, an airport in London, or their home. This flexibility is a not "perk" they are hoping to get from their employer. This is the way they want to work and they are dictating the terms now. Employers are playing catch-up to adopt the technology tools that enable more efficient sourcing, vetting, and hiring and which reinvent the whole model of how work gets done that has been in place for over two hundred years. Not just leveraging the technology, but also looking at the model of getting work done that was limited and which operated on the premise of a static, full time workforce. That includes working within brick and mortar offices, at a set schedule, and a traditional career tract and hierarchical leadership style rather than a flat, team and network style of management. Many employers are struggling to adapt to not just how work gets done but also aligning their workforce planning and strategy to a workforce that is dynamic and fluid. They are having to look at and ask the question, "what is the right workforce mix?" They are also intrigued about the other possibilities. Can they outsource a role, or break it apart to be crowd sourced, or should their hire someone permanent? If they do want to select other talent supply options, there is confusion over how to leverage this workforce and integrate it in a way that drives the company forward and enables a high functioning, engaged total workforce. Finding that right fit talent has never been more complex; not just figuring out the right solution to get work done, but accommodating, engaging, retaining a workforce that wants to work on their terms, and be engaged in a way that suites their goals and passions, in a framework that provides the freedom and flexibility they are not only requesting but expecting.

So, despite this complexity and uncertainty, embracing this new employment construct and world of work makes good business sense. Many business analysts and industry experts are predicting half of the S&P 500 Companies will be replaced in the next decade because they are up against "unicorn" startups and have to accommodate constant market change and disruption. Organizational inertia is the biggest threat to companies today.

Adopting a workforce strategy that is fluid and flexible, and that enables a steady flow of new talent, innovation, and flexing with market changes will be the secret sauce to longevity. Leveraging a dynamic talent supply chain strategy is a competitive differentiator; we will talk about why.

Chapter 6: How You Can Leverage The Gig Workforce To Dominate In Your Industry

> *"There is nothing more difficult to take in hand, more perilous to conduct, or more uncertain in its success, than to take the lead in the introduction of a new order of things." ~Niccolo Machiavelli*

Now that the game has changed for how work gets done, where do companies begin to pull together all the components that make up the new normal in the gig economy for their workforce strategy? Why would they want to? It would mean taking a different view of the various supply channels, the technology that enables and connects this workforce, new workforce models, and new talent and recruitment strategies. I have had many conversations with clients around a desire and curiosity to hire the gig workforce, they see the value and how it can change their organization for the better. However, there is still a lot of confusion around when and how to use this workforce? Or why to use this workforce.

Maybe the key is not to look for one end to end solution to manage your total talent supply? Maybe it's about changing the way you look at talent and workforce strategy? Because on the other side of that equation, the workforce is changing it for you. These workers are utilizing technology and several income streams to make a living. They are deciding to work longer, and wanting flexibility in how they work and where they work. We are moving from a manufacturing to a services economy. Many workers are shifting to a more "intraprenurial" mindset. They are okay working on a project for a year or less, or offering support for multiple clients.

So how does an organization piece together the different supplies of talent across a spectrum of permanent, contract, and independent consultant? How do they go beyond this to integrate the technology delivery system that is key to engaging this talent and incorporating that into a total workforce strategy that up until maybe ten years ago was primarily permanent talent?

This is the challenge many organizations are facing. Not only how to incorporate the different categories of worker, but deciding where, when and how they will use this workforce? When to hire a permanent worker, versus contractor, or independent consultant and for what role, project, or deliverable? Or do you need to hire anyone at all? Can you take that work and crowd source it?

The first step is, get ready for it... embracing that the traditional employment construct is over. Companies need to build from there. Yes, permanent employees will be a foundational part of any organization, however the traditional recruiting, sourcing model must undergo a radical change to stay competitive. And workforce planning and talent acquisition models must undergo a major overhaul, or be discarded entirely to compete in a more dynamic market.

Whoever embraces this new way of getting work done the fastest and most seamlessly wins; from a growth and revenue perspective as well as workforce retention and satisfaction. Talent is key to the longevity of any organization. And embracing a workforce and accommodating how they want to work is key to a happy productive workforce, particularly around flexibility.

Per The Insurance Journal's article; "Fluid Work as a Retention and Engagement Game-Changer: The Jacobson Group: April 2018" -offering alternative work environments can greatly improve employee satisfaction and even performance. The article goes on to say that this "fluidity" in your workforce approach is a key retention tool for many organizations; the flexibility and remote options are particularly attractive for those parents who struggle with child care. Allowing workers to choose how, where and why they want to work means lower turnover rates, higher engagement and higher revenues. Burnout has often been cited as a key turnover factor. By allowing for flexibility in your hiring practices, you can provide a just in time on demand workforce strategy that will prevent burnout from overworking key permanent talent.

There is a pragmatic talent recruitment and sourcing component as well. Using alternative talent supply chain strategies has the potential to vastly widen the talent pool — opening the field up to non-local professionals. Potential candidates no longer have to relocate for a job if they can work from home all or most days of the week. With flexible start and end times, working parents can schedule their jobs around childcare needs.

Attracting a broader scope of talent through flexible work could slow the impact of the aging workforce and make the industry more competitive in the job market. As we discussed earlier, they are the fastest growing population in the gig workforce. Providing options to keep them in the workforce will only strengthen a company's position and ability to be agile.

With consistent performance measurement, many young professionals thrive in a remote or fluid work environment. For forward-thinking organizations trying to accommodate a modern workplace and remain attractive to top talent, a flexible and fluid workplace strategy is a game-changer.

There are hundreds of articles (so won't quote any more here) written about the key to a company's longevity and growth being high workforce satisfaction and retention rates. Happy, Productive workers = Bigger profits. Always. The challenge for many organizations is how are workers today defining what makes them "happy?" Fifty years ago, it was a steady paycheck with a reputable and stable company. Anyone who binged watched Madmen saw this in action. You get the corner office, the expense account and you've arrived. Whether you were happy or fulfilled was not really part of the equation, it wasn't factored in. Those times are over, organizations are now focusing on the individual, what motivates you, makes you happy, and keeps you at a company?

There are two pieces to the equation in how enabling a gig workforce is key to a company's growth and domination in their market.

The first piece is the worker; we stated earlier, the vast majority of the gig workforce is choosing to participate in the gig workforce and some of your best talent can only be found in these communities.

As stated earlier this workforce is statistically more engaged and happy; they are working on their terms with the flexibility and freedom that makes these roles so attractive. They also are strongly incented to perform because of the fact there is no guarantee of income. You don't have to go through the long, drawn out process of terminating someone like you do with an employee. No 90 day probation period, written warnings, meetings with HR. You simply terminate their contract. In many ways, workers find this less risky. Their employment and continuation is based strictly on merit and what they produce. The false safety of a permanent job can be much more mercurial in when organizations retain and fire people. The economy, mergers, personality conflicts, budget cuts, are all factors an employee has little to no control over. A gig worker creates their own market and marketability with their in-demand skill sets and experience. For many this feeling of control, such as it is, makes this a very attractive option. "Stable" employment is becoming an outdated notion, as the "stability" comes more and more into question. A lot has changed since the "Great Recession"; massive layoffs and eliminating entire job categories have changed our traditional view of work. Employees are disenchanted with the Corporate Lifestyle. The ideal of long and stressful days, poor work/life balance and salaries not keeping pace with inflation is no longer attractive. As more companies make cuts, and burn out employees, workers want to take matters into their own hands.

To make it clear; I am not disparaging the need and place for permanent workforce. There will always be the need for that foundation; the "nucleus" of a company. C-Suite, long time employees who are guardians of the culture, those are important roles. However, the structure of organizations' workforce is permanently changed. Allowing more fluidity and agility into your workforce structure is key to longevity for a company, particularly in today's business climate, with constant threats from outside "unicorn" startups that do whatever you do only smarter, faster. Technology, Block Chain and AI are making it easier for companies to dominate by leveraging these powerful tools. Some are still in their infancy stage but make no mistake, the time is coming where some of the monoliths Fortune 100/500 companies will start to fall and will be replaced by (or minimized by) smaller, smarter, bleeding edge competitors. Globalization of the workforce and multinational expansion with few barriers or low barrier of entry into new markets means companies will need to be more agile than ever. Key to that agility and market domination is the right talent strategy. Without a workforce, you don't have a company. The best talent provides the best solutions. The organization that can attract and retain the best talent will win the market. Without energetic, creative teams, the business will lose the competitive race; the best talent brings the best ideas.

So wouldn't it make sense, for a company that needs to embrace agility, innovation, creativity and ability to adapt to different market conditions, to go with a workforce that mirrors that?

Maybe the way to look at this is to ask whether the gig workforce is exploding at exactly the right time to accommodate the changing market conditions and business climate. Which came first...? It's hard to tell.

Leveraging the gig workforce has solid practical applications in a business environment. It provides an agile workforce strategy to accommodate market peaks and valleys. I have seen this often in manufacturing. I had a client who of their many products, they manufactured floor heaters; their high peak season just before the winter months would slow down to a crawl in the spring. They had to triple their production staff during the peak then had no work in the spring. They used almost all contract labor; with a handful of permanent staff; plant manager, finance, foreman, and a few full time production machinists. This flexibly allowed them to meet production deadlines and maintain a solid profitability (given labor is usually the highest cost in any endeavor). It also preserved the jobs of the "core" permanent employees.

Despite the different advocacy groups and politicians talking about the loss of social safety net for this workforce (benefits, and other protections offered employees) this growth in the gig workforce appears to be a natural fit for how we want to work and changes in the business climate. It's the next step in the evolutionary process in the world of work.

In fact, the Gig economy is reinventing the social safety net, not destroying it. The lack of "Social Safety Net" for these workers is the last 'fig leaf' to remove before we totally embrace this new world of work. That argument is starting to crumble as I write this chapter.

With these shifts, here's how the Gig Economy is taking care of its own:

1. **Technology App and Service Providers are stepping up to provide a new social safety net with portable, tailored benefits and insurance.** However many organizations are not aware of this, so workers and employers alike are still struggling to navigate through the maze of choices. Companies like BenefitFocus are stepping up to provide benefits for those not eligible for employer medical – (such as the gig economy, 1099 employees, etc.) to select, purchase and maintain a diverse set of plans. Per Jeff Oldham SVP "Gig economy workers, due either to the variability of their work hours and/or because they are 1099 employees, cannot rely on "payroll deductions" to purchase benefits. Similar to ecommerce sites, the incorporation of credit cards and third-party payment platforms (e.g. Apple Pay, PayPal, and Amazon Wallet) is the new norm." These benefits are cost effective and flexible.

Our government is also catching up; slowly. Senator Mark Warner (D-VA) and U.S. Rep. Suzan DelBene (D-WA) introduced legislation designed to evaluate innovative portable benefit designs for the growing independent workforce. The twenty million dollar grant fund within the U.S. Department of Labor encourages states, cities and non-profits to come up with new portable benefit models which provide independent workers with health care, retirement plans, life or disability insurance, sick leave, training and educational benefits.

2. **Gig Workforce Technology Providers are Partnering with other Agencies to provide Gig Worker Support services – that accommodate the way they work.** These agencies are seeing the opportunity to partner with gig workforce technology companies to provide an ecosystem of support. Per Keith Clithero; founder of Gig Connected a mobile-friendly web application that provides direct access to a pool of skilled and unskilled workers for commercial, residential, or highway and road construction projects. "We are a connector for the construction community for organizations like Urban League, Charlotte Works, NC Works NextGEN, Urban Ministries and many more. They are doing incredible work on staffing, workforce development and training includingfinance basics;

avoiding check cashing places, and providing ancillary support services to the blue-collar workforce."

3. **Providing a broad and steady range of flexible opportunities and multiple income streams that were non-existent ten years ago.** The ways of earning a living have changed radically with the gig and "sharing economy". There are new avenues to make money for those that have an entrepreneurial spirit. Take the Uber driver who had a prison record; albeit fifteen years ago, and many companies would not give him a job, even with his spotless record post release. Uber did, and he made seventy thousand dollars a year and was proud of his 4.9 Uber rating with over five thousand trips. He drove fifteen hours most days, long day yes but was happy and proud of his accomplishment. He had the freedom, flexibility and an income stream available that worked for him.

While the nature of work is changing rapidly, our worker protection policies largely remain tied to a twentieth century model of traditional full-time employment. A model that many are now shunning willingly to work independently and offer their services, skills and experience on terms that better fit the way they want to live, work and contribute to the world.

Another interesting trend that will help companies change their game is the growth of the aging population in the gig economy as I mentioned earlier. "Baby Boomers" and "Traditionalists" is an untapped treasure in talent. They are the fastest growing population in the gig economy. Per Deloitte's Article; "No time to retire - Redesigning work for our aging workforce" Dec 18 ***TODAY'S FASTEST-GROWING*** *workforce segment is taking organizations by storm—wanting flexibility, equal opportunities, and better access to training and development. They are asking for deeper meaning in their work and looking to make societal impacts that transcend their own footprint. And no, we are not talking about millennials. We are talking about employees working well into their 70s, forging their way into uncharted territory and redefining what it means to be an aging worker.*

The article goes on to say that this generation has more grit, higher engagement levels, better relationship buildings skills and experience than their younger peers. So there's a big kick in the pants to every ageist recruiter.

Surprisingly, the article also stated *while stereotypes about age-related rigidity and cognitive decline abound, research shows that age and core task performance are largely unrelated.*[24] *In fact, certain skills that can help older workers provide unique value to their organizations, such as social skills, can actually improve as we age.*[25] *In addition, studies have also shown that older workers can be just as creative and innovative as younger employees.[26]And while speed and the ability to multitask tend to decline after age fifty-five, mature workers often display a great deal of wisdom, which can lead them to make more realistic judgments than some younger people do.[27]*

And surprisingly, older workers can help attract older customers; a big benefit for companies catering to an aging population. As our population is living longer and healthier lives, it is quite conceivable to work well into your seventies or even eighties.

This all comes down to rethinking everything you know about how works gets done. Not only the type of talent and how they are engaged, but also where they sit geographically, their age, and taking apart and rebuilding the traditional employment construct that fits the way we work today.

Expanding your talent strategy to multiple talent supply options is key to staying competitive, particularly in a tightening labor market. A company's growth and profitability is dependent on customer satisfaction, staying relevant in the market, and revenue growth. Talent is key to this directive. The right talent, at the right time.

The HR, CEO, COO or Talent Acquisition leader who is part of enabling an effective workforce strategy would be ahead of the game by educating themselves and understanding the gig workforce, the technology enablers, and how people work today. The gig workforce is not a necessary evil or to a tool to provide "fill in" talent for temporary projects, workers on leave, or a "warm body" for lesser roles when you can't find permanent talent.

The key to leveraging an effective gig workforce strategy is embracing and effectively integrating all the talent supply channels available and understanding how each work and where they work within the organization. (Or you can hire my firm and we will help you).

It's about having the right ecosystem of talent supply (staffing providers, gig workforce platforms, permanent recruitments, and crowd sourcing sties) then having a strategy that dictates how they will all fit together within your organization. It's about having an organizational culture that understands the value of this workforce and having a more agile approach to how work gets done.

It's also about those few brave souls that will lead their organization into having a solid strategy for introducing a way of work and talent supply that many are reluctant to embrace because they don't understand the value or have preconceived notions of the quality of this talent. We have seen many of our clients have success this way; by having some smaller wins with a particular department and it takes off from there. Grass roots; ground up versus top down "from the ivory tower."

Throughout this book we will give you a road map on how to do this, why you want to do this and how it will benefit your organization. We have spelled out all the shifts and changes that have created and been the catalyst for this new world of work, and given birth to the gig economy.

In the next chapter we will give you some tips to build and integrate a solid gig workforce strategy. This will ensure your organization thrives in the new world of work and ensure you have the best talent strategy which is key to dominating your industry.

Chapter 7: How To Leverage The Gig Workforce Effectively And Where They Fit Into Your Organization

How does this workforce fit in with your traditional talent strategy? What is the best way to leverage this workforce as a competitive differentiator?

So where to begin?

The biggest areas of confusion are around when to use this workforce and where is it most effective? Questions like when do I use a permanent person versus a gig worker? To start, you have to implement the technology and processes to accommodate the sourcing, on boarding, managing, and quality control for these workers. Then integrate the whole strategy into a total talent management approach. Total Talent management is an aspirational desire at this moment. Many Staffing and Workforce Solution providers promise a seamless integration of all talent, technology and HRIS systems but that has been much more challenging than anticipated. The reason: most companies have not caught up to the changes in the new normal workforce landscape. They are grappling with how to integrate multiple technologies, change their recruiting and sourcing processes to accommodate a multi-talent supply strategy, and deal with the cultural bias and resistance to using more of this workforce. There are some step by step processes I can share with you to make this happen (aka free consulting; and a big thank you for buying this book.)

Here is a step by step process to integrating an effective gig workforce strategy for any company at any stage in their talent acquisition strategy.

1. **Start with your HR and Talent Acquisition department on understanding what a Total Workforce solution looks like.** HR Leaders are being asked to step away from traditional roles of risk management and collecting yearly performance reviews (which are also on their way out by the way, but that's another discussion). They are being asked to be a strategic player at the table and an advisor, to navigate new technologies, manage employee expectations, and ensure the organization has a productive and happy workforce. HR leaders are now interacting with leaders across the organization; because high quality talent is a number one priority. HR leaders are tasked with implementing end-to-end talent management solutions that meet the requirements of large, complex organizations. There needs to be more collaboration and input from the organization on what the specific workforce needs are, the projects to be completed. HR and Talent leaders need to be a critical part

of this overall workforce planning. HR transformation is a priority at a very high level. The organization of the future is a top priority for companies. I think that one of the challenges is a lot of HR organizations are behind the curve in addressing key enterprise issues, including talent alignment, skill shortages and organizational change. The days of emailing several permanent reqs. requests to be filled to a Talent Acquisition team are not enough. It needs to be a more strategic level discussion on the solution around workforce mix, project planning, and there needs to be more collaboration.

2. **HR leaders need to educate themselves on the different workforce options available and the best fit for each.** Hiring a primarily permanent workforce is no longer going to be a solution in the near future. Organizations need to look at the holistic mix of how work gets done; automation, AI, Independent Consultants, Contractors, Crowd Sourcing. Other leaders within the organization have to be a part of these discussions to decide what makes the most sense. How to best obtain all outcomes? The answer is not always to hire a permanent worker. Leveraging the gig workforce is not about cost saving measures or getting out of paying benefits. It's not about getting a "temporary fix" until you can find someone permanent. It's about embracing a completely different way of getting work done and getting

used to the fact that your workforce makeup is radically changing.

3.   **Use a Bottom up Approach to "Test Drive" integrating Gig Workers into your workforce mix,** especially if it's unfamiliar to many in your organization and particularly if you are using technology (that is, an on-demand workforce technology platform like Upwork or Catalant) as the delivery system. See graphic below:

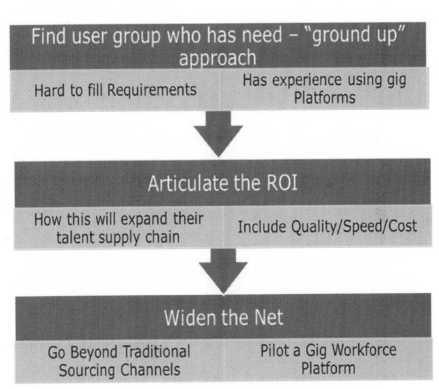

Find user group who has need – "ground up" approach

| Hard to fill Requirements | Has experience using gig Platforms |

Articulate the ROI

| How this will expand their talent supply chain | Include Quality/Speed/Cost |

Widen the Net

| Go Beyond Traditional Sourcing Channels | Pilot a Gig Workforce Platform |

Using a bottom up approach does a couple things. It helps you to engage the enterprise and make them part of the solution. Otherwise, pushing down a mandate to use more gig workers "from the ivory tower" known as "corporate" never works and builds resistance. You can also pilot this with one or two groups that meet the criteria above then use the wins from that pilot to roll out to the rest of the organization if you want to move to a more fluid workforce. It depends on where your organization is in the adoption curve of more progressive workforce solutions.

4.   **Make Technology your Friend- it's the delivery system for the Gig Workforce.** The biggest challenge is businesses trying to figure out the mix of technology and services. Over the past three years, gig workforce platforms have been ramping up their services, from pretty much just technology to adding services add-ons. This is a hard thing for technology firms to do, for a lot reasons. But increasingly, businesses really don't just want technology (like they did in the eighties). Now technology has really become a service, and people do not think in terms of technology but rather what they get of value, delivered through technology. And what they get tends to involve some mix of humans and technology.

This means getting your technology department engaged to determine how these technology platforms will fit in with your other HRIS and vendor and spend management systems (like VMS Technology, Procurement systems). The good news is gig workforce platforms are built with easy integration in mind and many are cloud based requiring no actual implementation. Other complimentary services, that are technology based, like independent consultant vetting and indemnification services, talent cloud platforms, are also built specifically with integration in mind, and they are all very compatible with common HRIS and other Talent Technology. In general, all HR and Talent Technology providers are designing their systems with compatibility with other related technology systems. Today it's about custom technology ecosystems rather than monolithic, rigid big box technology solutions that are too big and unwieldy to accommodate the multiple technology solutions that make up modern talent acquisition.

5. **Use Metrics and use Feedback to track progress.** This will be your foundation for the business case to integrate different talent supply channels into your total workforce strategy. Capture metrics that are compelling to the business such as fill rates, retention rates, worker quality and cost. There are some benefits that are typical of the gig workforce in addition to flexibility. There are also substantial cost savings and speed to fill (which negates productivity losses due to positions going unfilled). Leveraging a gig workforce has

to add value to the organization. Mandates never work, you often have a reluctant user base and the fact you had to mandate the use of a type of talent supply or technology negates the validity of that choice. It implies there is a reason you have to mandate (i.e. use this or else Corp. will not be happy) that someone "cheapens" the solution. I was having this conversation the other day with a client who is a procurement executive for a large financial services company. He was frustrated that he had to implement a contingent workforce strategy and technology for a department that didn't want it, who wanted to continue doing "their own thing" and the company refused to "mandate" use of this solution. I told him that was a good thing; the LAST thing he wanted to do was mandate this strategy as it would be a lost cause out of the gate. No one wants to feel their terms of how they conduct their business are being forced on them and it cheapens the solution. Ultimately the solution has to add value. If it adds value and makes their life easier, no mandating required. The way to add value is to listen to the business, find out what their pain points are and solve for it.

Understanding how and when to leverage different levers in your talent supply chain can make the difference between a Talent Acquisition/HR department being seen as an asset to business strategy and driving bottom line results or it being seen as simply a steward of outdated corporate policy. Please don't take offense for any HR Leaders reading; I am stating a big of a cliché. Ultimately it is about understanding the needs of your business and finding a talent strategy the delivers high quality, cost effective talent, on time and within budget. That is the secret sauce for any HR or Talent Acquisition leader to be seen as value adding by the organization.

The biggest challenge is many businesses and organizations are very much attached to an older paradigm of how work gets done, as detailed in earlier chapters. Many organizations are having to circumvent outdated processes of hiring and recruiting; non-technology enabled job posting approvals, resume review, screening, vetting, and on boarding. The most imposing challenge is time as these outdated processes move too slowly for today's worker. A strong candidate has too many options today to work the way they want to. The outdated methods of making a candidate wait for weeks while their resume is mulled over and reviewed by HR, the department head, hiring manager, then a couple more weeks of multiple interviews, then a few weeks after that to hear back (or not hear at all) are over. Operating this way is not going to cut it when technology speeds everything up and puts a lot of power and information in a candidate's hands. They can see how many positions you have open on Indeed, go on your site and apply for jobs then judge you on how quickly you respond and engage, see how your employees feel about working there on Glassdoor, look at your financials, your social media accounts and read what is being written by you and about you by your employees on twitter. All of this can be done in minutes. While you are mulling over their resume and spending weeks to set up an interview, they have already completely scanned you, made an assessment, got scouted for a consulting gig that starts in Paris and entertaining other offers from bots working with multiple recruiting networks representing other companies who move faster than you. You have already been eliminated as a potential place to work.

I read a tweet from a woman yesterday whose husband was downsized from Tesla after they cut back on staff. She stated that he was a disabled veteran, got no severance, no notice and they are now desperate. She threw in a couple F-bombs for good measure. She had a twitter following of three hundred or so and yet her tweet went viral and last I looked had over ten thousand likes, shares, retweets. In an instant, the public got a micro view into a corporate culture (as perceived by one person). There are no more secrets and there is more transparency on both sides of the equation; the person being engaged or employed and the one doing the hiring or engaging. Social media and the internet of things has completely changed the hiring and recruiting process. Those that don't embrace the new world of work, and new workforce models will be left behind.

Maybe things will change once the looming recession hits. I am not an economist and far as I can tell even the economists have no clue when or where a recession will hit. Just before the Great Recession many economists were talking about favorable market conditions, growth in new home building, just before the floor fell out. I personally believe economists are like weather men (or women).They are both just as accurate. And if any economists bought my book and are reading this now, I do respect what you do and no offense intended. However, we are heading towards a recession. Some saying this one will be more severe than the great recession because of global conditions in slowing growth and inflation, trade war, technology and automation replacing jobs, etc. The list goes on and on. However, what does not appear to be changing is the fact that demand for talent exceeds supply and many are saying, going into the recession this will still be the case. So what does that look like? The country (or world) is in a recession but jobs are still plentiful and competitive? Companies will need to adapt to stay profitable. Many will go into cost cutting mode to stay alive and will be forced to look at their most expensive expenditure; talent. It's always the most costly overhead in any company. So in addition to embracing more organic changes in how we work, the world of work, and the explosive growth in the gig workforce, there will be economic pressure to expedite that path of using this workforce. Of looking at labor costs more strategically and what is the most profitable way to get work done? This combined with a growing focus on what attracts, retains, and enables a highly productive workforce will only help solidify a different approach of how work gets done.

A Recession would only expedite trends already taking place. We will move more aggressively towards shifting away from hiring for job titles and labor types and focusing on work product and outcomes and align a sourcing and recruiting strategy around that. We will look at how does the talent want to work and have connecting mechanisms for different types of talent; perm, gig, part time, throughout the talent supply chain. Per Michael Arena; Chief Talent Officer for General Motors. He suggests "removing the walls of insularity" between permanent and gig talent and making it about "talent" in all its forms. He goes on to say in an interview with John Healy; Vice President and Managing Director of Kelly Service's Interview "Is Temporary the New Permanent" talent, that you need to constantly invest in "new thinking" to "build the bridge to the outside world" and ensure innovation and creativity continues to flow through the organization via all forms of talent, permanent and nontraditional.

This comment from a relatively established company, General Motors, known more for its traditional corporate environment and trying to survive in an embattled industry is a sign of changing times. Companies are starting to rethink how they build their workforce; where they will get the talent, how they will leverage the talent. Companies see the value of leveraging the gig workforce and they are hungering for counsel and guidance in how to incorporate this workforce into the more traditional models and processes that exist in their companies today.

This approach will be even more important in tough economic conditions; where weaknesses will be exposed, and lack of innovation and fresh thinking will make you vulnerable. Companies need to start thinking today about how they are going to prepare for the recession, and building out a new workforce structure, that is agile, flexible, cost effective and aligns with how talent wants to work will be more important than ever. It is this foresight and forward thinking that will insulate companies in a severe economic downturn and ensure they not only survive but thrive.

As we mentioned earlier, a crucial component to embracing this new world of work is focusing more on outcomes and work products versus job roles and titles. As organizations become flatter, and career tenures become shorter and more diverse, organizations need to rethink how work gets done and build a multi- talent supply chain strategy around that. This means looking at your current workforce planning processes and getting your HR and Talent Acquisition teams to sit down with department heads and look beyond allotting headcount to projects and divisions. It involves getting them to look instead at how the work can get done within the talent continuum. Can you plan in some fluidity and flexibility into some of the work streams and resource needs? Odds are you already have this in place, albeit fragmented across departments and divisions.

Most organizations have already embraced leveraging non-traditional labor. They are already using contractors, independent consultants, and talent cloud sourcing sites. The challenge is they are not using these workers as part of a larger workforce planning approach. It is more ad hoc. So HR and Talent Acquisition leaders are tasked with bringing these disparate talent supply chains together in a cohesive way as part of an overall total talent and workforce strategy approach. Often, as stated earlier, you can leverage best practices from other departments regarding the usage of non-traditional labor and start to build the framework of process, technology and systems and integrate that into your total workforce planning. You already have the beginning of a bottom up approach that is often the catalyst for bigger changes.

The good news is most organizations can use the technologies and processes they have in place now with a few adjustments.

Key to embracing a multi-talent strategy is to start with having the delivery system to provide multiple channels of traditional and non-traditional talent in a way that is embraced by the organization. The key to that approach is to keep disruption to a minimum. Leverage what technologies and systems you have in place today where possible. Most companies have a delivery system for contract labor; either with more managed solutions leveraging a Vendor Management System (VMS) or using staffing providers to bring in contract labor. How are you leveraging your staffing providers? Many of them have workforce solution options beyond contract placement; and they know your business inside and out. Leveraging your staffing providers more strategically could get you some quick wins as well. All gig workforce on demand technology platforms can be easily integrated into your Vendor Management System (most have partnerships or integrations with this technology) and this technology becomes the delivery system to introduce freelancers, independent consultants, and talent clouds into an existing channel that delivers other contract labor. If you don't have a Vendor Management System (VMS), that's okay as most gig workforce technology platforms can be set up as standalone and cloud based. Before some of you ask "What is the cloud and what does that have to do with on boarding new talent?" The Cloud concept is not new and has been around for years within Technology. Per Balaji Ramanujim; CIO for Tatum (A Randstad Company). "The Cloud has helped tap into underutilized hardware assets and SaaS helped tap into underutilized software assets to realize new business possibilities. Further, allowing IT to tap into human talent and other surrounding underutilized assets is a natural progression. Imagine an IT platform that is not only aware of all the supply and demand, but also the manifold ways in which supply can be dynamically reshaped or transformed to meet changing demand. And that's where the Gig platform is headed."

Similar to downloading Spotify. You can use these technologies as needed; and many also have other bundled services such as IC vetting and indemnification services along with employer of record services to mitigate co-employment risk, invoicing and payment processing, so that you have a fully contained solution to augment your existing contract staffing labor with other types of non-traditional talent. If you already have a population of independent consultants you are bringing on ad hoc, you can enable the growth and integration of this workforce further by putting some risk mitigation processes around it to ensure maximum usage without risk. There are many solution providers that offer a menu of services to accommodate your independent workforce; indeminification, Agent or Employer of record, invoicing and payment processes.

An Employer's on boarding process can be tweaked to accommodate non-traditional talent. Many gig workers will be tasked with delivering work products remotely versus coming into the office every day. Most of them have their own equipment (laptop, cell phone, etc.). However, they may need to have access to your network so what does that look like? "This new trend in worker/employer relationships is causing many of our clients to review their teleworker policies. Specifically, what IT access (cellular, Internet and data) is needed to help the workers be as productive as possible?" Says Tom Reda, VP of Marketing for The Profit Advisory Group, a company that helps other companies reduce their telecomm costs and eliminate waste and erroneous charges.

So integrating an effective gig workforce strategy comes down to two major components; changing your approach on how you view work getting done; moving away from employee centric and incorporating the technology, processes and alternative talent supply channels we discussed.

The most challenging aspect is embracing this new normal of a fluid workforce. The processes, technology, operational models already exist. Once you embrace alternative work models and help others in your organization to embrace it and understand the value, the rest is tactical. Changing a culture and beliefs and attraction and retention strategy is much trickier. Your organization will need to see proof that that non-traditional talent can deliver, are reliable, and don't necessarily have to be sitting next to you or even in the same city, state or country to contribute meaningfully to your team, project, organization. Once biases and misperceptions around how effectively leveraging the gig workforce can positively impact an organization are changed, then it's a matter of implementing an effective multi talent supply strategy.

As we described earlier, all of the components; technology providers, gig workforce platforms, IC Risk Management, pay rolling, invoicing, VMS, Staffing providers; are all already seeing the value of collaboration and ecosystems to deliver comprehensive multi talent supply strategies for clients. This approach has been core to our service offering at Gallagher; an ecosystem of providers coming together with technology API and integrations, to deliver end to end, a gig workforce strategy or really a total talent strategy. The lines are being blurred more every year between gig, perm, part-time. Now it's just about talent. Total Talent.

Technology has come up often throughout this chapter and the reason for that is Technology is the biggest catalyst for the change in how we work and the explosive growth of the gig economy. Not just because it's the delivery system, payment vehicle, vetting, sourcing, evaluating mechanism, but it's also become the truth teller with Blockchain stepping into the arena. Blockchain, AI, and Machine Learning has been coming to the forefront in this sector and many don't understand it or throw the terms around loosely to look cool and innovative. Everybody has AI, and Machine Learning in their marketing materials but connecting reality to fantasy are two different things. As with everything in life; it comes down to execution and that is where the metal meets the road. Ideas are not execution. We will now take a deeper dive into the Technology aspect of the gig economy and will be delighted to separate fact from fiction.

Chapter 8: What Are The Technology Changes Enabling The Integration Of This Workforce?

"Every once in a while, a new technology, an old problem, and a big idea turn into an innovation." ~ Dean Kamen

"Block chain systems offer the possibility for each of us to become free agents who collaborate on projects, get paid for what we contribute and have the quality of our work assessed by peers and clients. In other words, no bosses. "Nix the C-suite, Soon Block chain will let armies of Free agents run Companies" – CNBC April 2018

The article goes on to say that the key to this new "future of work" system is based on trusted reputation scores built upon the experiences of colleagues, collaborators and clients and accumulated over a lifetime of project contribution, all secured by a Blockchain to guarantee accuracy, immutability and personal control over your own data. In essence, this allows for trust between individuals to scale to global levels. Blockchains remove the need for third party intermediaries (anyone ranging from Visa, to colleges, to the DMV) whose role is to attest to the accuracy of any statement that, with verification, facilitates trust. It's the difference between someone saying, "I was a key player on Project X" and having a sworn affidavit from a client and a boss that says, 'John was a key player on Project X."

In short, Blockchain enables the rating, vetting, deploying and paying of independent workers all within the organization. Decentralized Autonomous Organizations can be set up and set rules for behavior, collective decision-making, funding, governance, hiring and firing. Those rules can be enforced without the need for a procurement officer, HR, accounts payable or marketing.

With 70 percent of people disengaged at work, many people would prefer an alternative to the status quo. Supported by systems of global trust, secured by blockchains, the day may soon come where you are able to do more of what you are really good at and get paid for it, all without a boss.

Many of these technology companies can be integrated into existing HRIS systems and are being designed with collaboration in mind. Basically, any step in the talent supply chain end to end, for perm and gig, can be automated or enabled by technology, end to end. All the participants within this technology ecosystem are figuring out that it makes more sense to build integration or collaboration friendly technology that customers can "plug into" their existing systems or use standalone to help with recruiting and sourcing. Many companies are using many of these technology companies; on-demand gig workforce platforms, talent cloud providers, vendor management systems, recruitment marketplace, E-staffing, Job Board Aggregators, and on and on; are seeing the value and simplicity of using these firms. For most, there is no intensive deployment or implementation. The costs are usually subscription based or per transaction, and you don't have the big dollar software purchases, licensing, add-ons, and implementation costs you have with some of the more traditional technology solutions. There is an agility to a talent technology ecosystem that actually adds simplicity rather than complexity. Complexity comes from trying to accommodate rigid technology platforms that don't have the configurability and open approach to work within a technology ecosystem for talent. Companies then end up building workarounds, and elaborate processes, which add to the complexity. Less is not more, less is restrictive and rigid.

Cloud enabled solutions mean that you can have an ecosystem of Talent and Gig Workforce Technology providers to enable the sourcing and on boarding of gig workers, lifecycle management of on boarding thru off boarding, invoicing, and payments,

Advancements in technology are changing nearly everything about the way people work across various industries, and this transformation also pertains to the inner workings of talent acquisition.

A shift toward a more integrated approach to workforce planning is currently underway due to talent scarcity, a widening of the skills gap and improved access to technology. HR and Talent Acquisition Leaders are anticipated to go on "a tech buying spree to get better access to talent."

Technology advancements are expected to accelerate the sourcing and on-boarding of new talent that can lead their companies to undergo desired transformation. Jason Roberts, global head of talent analytics and technology for the Talent Innovation Center at Randstad, said "there is only a limited value to attempting to combat talent scarcity by adding to the number of recruiters involved." "To make a truly transformational impact on talent acquisition, you need to invest in the tools that most effectively empower your people and processes," states Roberts.

Analytics dashboards and AI-related tools have impacted the ways in which many HR professionals do their recruitment work in recent years and most companies are expected to invest significantly toward accelerating these talent choices. There will be a shift for HR Leaders to view their role in building flexible workforces and establishing talent models as crucial. Technology is enabling business leaders to take on a "total talent" approach and employers are thinking more broadly about techniques for completing necessary work both through traditional and unconventional methods.

The biggest challenge is how organizations are accommodating these changes in technology. I think the quality is high for these technology providers and it is continuing to evolve, but productivity has not caught up.

I come across clients all the time who have had WorkDay or some other HRIS system implemented but do not have the aftercare/support needed. They don't understand the technology or how to integrate it into their business fully once implemented. It's like giving the keys to a Dodge Viper after someone just got their license. I see a role as an "after care" specialist to provide support post-launch to help them leverage functionality and features and integrate them into their day-to-day life. In many ways, if done right, technology implementation is never really "done." It just shifts to after care and optimization to continue to support and optimize the business. Sometimes, it's a matter of knowing what to "turn on." In a lot of cases, after implementation is done, the team that does the implementation leaves and the client really doesn't know how to use their new technology. Then you add other cloud based Talent Technology; on demand and gig workforce platforms, Talent Clouds, Vendor Management systems who in many cases are far more advanced than legacy "big box" technology solutions.

HR transformation and Talent Acquisition is a priority at a very high level. The organization of the future is a top priority for companies. The biggest thing from a cost perspective is prioritizing what solutions are needed first, addressing legacy systems, and talent recruitment. I think that one of the challenges is that a lot of HR organizations are behind the curve in addressing key enterprise issues, including talent alignment, skill shortages and organizational change. And they don't have the expertise or experience to make complex technology decisions. And getting their CIO and Technology leadership involved is a challenge; they have too many other priorities to dedicate resources.

Most HR organizations are simply too busy fighting fires to get out in front on strategic issues. In many cases, they are in reactive mode, with too much on their plate and an inability to say "no" to work that does not allow HR to become more strategic.

So even with all of these technology advancements in Total Talent Management and Engaging non-traditional labor to make lives easier, for many HR leaders it just adds to the complexity and an already overwhelmed work load.

So many changes in such a short period of time! No wonder organizations are confused. The challenge begins with shifting to a new model of how work gets done, moving beyond traditional sourcing and permanent roles to embrace a more fluid workforce. That in itself is a big hurdle. Then HR, Procurement and Talent Leaders, need to look at the delivery system and enabler; which is technology for this alternative workforce. Then figure out how all of these components fit together to ensure an engaged, productive, happy workforce.

So let's start with the basics; and the types of technology enabling the new world of work.

Talent Technology	What is Does	Examples
Job Boards	Designed to allow employers to post job requirements for a position to be filled. I think most companies use them for data now; do people still use job boards?	Dice, Monster, Ladders
On-Demand Workforce Platforms	Flexible labor marketplace, enabled by technology where buyers can obtain temporary labor for all manner of tasks and jobs	Catalant, Tilr, Fiverr
Recruitment Marketplace	On-Demand Recruiting platform that enables companies to outsource their talent recruitment to a network of recruiters to find talent	RecruitLoop, Talent Crowd, Bounty Jobs
Candidate Relationship Management	A method for managing and improving relationships with current and potential future job candidates. CRM technology is used to automate communication process with the candidates, encourage their engagement and improve candidate experience.	PhenomPeople, Clinch, TalentBrew
Behavioral Assessment	Enables candidates to take variety of behavioral and other tests via an app or online that are scored based on pre-identified attributes; aids in the pre-hire process.	Knack, Pymetrics, Chemistry
Vendor Management Systems	An Internet-enabled, often Web-based application that acts as a mechanism for business to manage and procure staffing services – temporary, and, in some cases, permanent placement services – as well as outside contract or contingent labor.	Vndly, Coupa, SimplifyVMS
ATS (Applicant Tracking Systems)	Software application that enables the electronic handling of recruitment needs. An ATS can be implemented or accessed online on an enterprise or small business level, depending on the needs of the company.	ADP, Jobvite, WorkDay
Freelancer Management Systems	Centralized repository for hiring, project, and payroll management for businesses employing freelancers, contractors, or independent consultants. Freelance management systems oversee the entire freelancer relationship—from finding a freelancer to measuring their performance.	GigWalk, Freelancer, MBO Partners

So the big question is; how do all these systems fit together? Where do you start? As an employer or as a worker? Because that is what this technology is all about; bringing the two together. Ultimately, this is about putting people to work; and enabling people to work the way they want to, when they want to and where they want to.

The above are small sample of examples of the different types of Talent Technology. At its simplest, it's about finding the talent where they sit (Job Boards, On-Demand Workplace), leveraging ways to find the talent (recruitment marketplace), vetting the talent (Candidate relationship Management and Behavioral assessment) on boarding and tracking (ATS) and Managing talent, (Contract Labor – VMS). The lines are being blurred between permanent and the gig workforce. This ecosystem of technology is growing to accommodate all components of sourcing, hiring, vetting, on boarding, paying for this talent. There are also complimentary technology and solution providers that are also supporting this ecosystem of technology to enable the usage of independent consultants (IC's); providing IC indemnification, invoicing, support, and "connector" technology to integrate these systems into expanded technology that touches workforce systems; that is, purchasing and procurement systems that cover invoicing, financials, purchase orders. Other HRIS Technology platforms. Particularly for non-permanent labor, the gig workforce is considered a buying "commodity" and often the "purchase" of this talent intersects with other systems. Per Dennis Kanegaye, Head of Global Alliances for Coupa Software (a global technology platform for Business Spend Management) who recently acquired a Vendor Management System platform; DCR. "We see the future of contract labor management as being 100% software driven with services eventually taking a back seat. We see managers being able to self-select their own contract and gig workers as needed using technology as the portal."

Technology and AI are not "replacing" or diminishing the roles of "the humans." It is removing non-value added tasks, freeing up our time and energy and enabling us to focus on new skills development, vital human relationships, strategic and critical thinking, and extending and enhancing the value of the overall delivery model.

Technology is the connector between all components of the new world of work and gig workers and permanent talent are being brought together via the different entry points technology provides. As more traditional "people" roles become automated; recruiting, scanning resumes, interviewing, sourcing, on boarding, the role of the human and technology will undergo massive shifts. There will be adjustments as we make room for technology to play a bigger role.

Another area Technology is having an impact in is Workforce Data and Analytics. With all of these tasks, transactions, lifecycle management, sourcing, vetting, evaluating of the workplace being enabled more and more by technology, that means the data around these events is being captured in an unprecedented way. Candidate feedback, worker profiles and performance, market rate and intel, sourcing, vetting, finding; all of these tasks and activities are now traceable. As stated earlier, Blockchain offers validation points that did not exist before. As the millennials say; there is no more privacy in the digital age.

The good news is you have more data than ever to help drive workforce performance and company growth. The bad news you have more data than ever and how do you read it, use it, and interpret it? It can be a tool or a weapon, depending on whose hands it sits in.

Some key trends to look out for in 2019 and beyond in Workforce Analytics:

~Per The HR Strategist; "What is Workforce Analytics and 6 Emerging Trends to Look out for in 2019" (Jan. 2019), some of the key ones that jumped out

1. **Analytics will transition from "one-time" to real time**. This will cover going beyond annual

employee surveys to more organic weekly/monthly/quarterly feedback with fewer questions. This concept could extend to ANY measurable data in HR and Workforce analytics as technology platforms that are cloud based enable access anytime, anywhere with many tools to aggregate and summarize the data.

2. **There will be greater focus on productivity.** This will go beyond just hiring new people when productivity slips (hint: it might be YOU Mr. or Mrs. Manager or Corporate Culture challenges). Data will help identify the key characteristic of top performing workers and establish a work environment fostering better performance.

3. **Data will shift from Individual Considerations to the wider network.** Workforce analytics will shift from focus on the individual on quality delivery to looking at groups, teams as a whole and moving towards organization network analysis.

4. **New tools will be available to help with application of this data and analysis.** A Deloitte report suggests that while seventy-five percent of companies believe in the importance of workforce analytics, only eight percent believe they are ready to embrace it. Companies need to have analytics experts and leverage state of the art tools and technologies to address these challenges.

Good data and analytics strategies are critical in the use of the gig workforce. Not just because they are part of the overall workforce, but because they fall outside much of the structure, protocol and systems that exists for permanent labor. This means that above all else visibility to spend, headcount, performance, costs is critical for effective workforce planning for the gig workforce. We have seen extreme example of this challenge with some of our clients. Clients that are spending one hundred million dollars or more a year on gig workforce and have no idea if this workforce is performing, where they are coming from, or if they are paying fair market rates. We worked with a fortune 100 digital and data Storage Company who was trying to get their arms around their contract labor and put in place some processes and technology to better manage that workforce. The Director of People Analytics could not pull a simple headcount report for all the contract labor in the company; there was no way to do it. The data was not captured and stored in a way that made that feasible.

The only way to accurately capture this data is to have this workforce captured in a data repository of some kind. A common approach to this is using a Vendor Management System (VMS) to manage the onboarding through offboarding of all gig workforce. Also many of the gig workforce platforms that provide independent and talent cloud workers usually have some basic reporting available to capture some of these foundational data points. The implementation of a VMS is easier than most think. Per Cheri Forbes, a VMS Project Management consultant; "you really only need a Project Manager and Solution Architect, and good client requirements to ensure a successful VMS implementation."

Technology is so intertwined with data because technology is the enabler and the repository of data for all facets of an organizations' workforce. Not just the quantitative in the form of headcount, costs, location, tenure, hiring trends. It is also qualitative in the form of worker performance for example. As discussed earlier, annual performance reviews are on their way out (thank God) and real time, 360 interactive feedback reviews are becoming more popular. The worker is also providing feedback on their experience with their management and corporate culture to spark more interactive dialog. There are technology platforms that now enable more dynamic feedback; like Capterra which also includes goal setting and compensation management. Technology is now helping to add a "warmer" touch by interacting more with potential candidates.

You also have candidate engagement tools that track visitors to your website who apply for jobs and ensure they always get some type of feedback or immediate engagement, even if it's with a bot. There are automated on boarding tools to expedite a candidate's start date; such as W9 forms, orientation, and training.

Technology is about SPEED. It is rapidly shortening the timeline from when a candidate first responds to an open position and when they are hired; from weeks and months to days. Time kills all deals; this is as said in sales and even more so when finding top talent. This is especially important in a hot job market when the best candidates are snatched up quickly. Some of this is because you are removing the humans from some (not all) of the equation. The humans that are usually working in Human Resources and Talent Acquisition are usually overburdened and burned out recruiters who don't have the time to screen, vet, schedule, and talk to all the possible candidates applying for a role. Technology is in essence providing a way to fill that gap and stay engaged with candidates and preventing them from slipping through the cracks. Technology helps to avoid some of the common issues that happen with overburdened HR departments; not being able to respond to a candidate who has interest. Or taking forever to schedule an interview, or lack of feedback after an interview. Or take a month or more to get back to a top candidate only to find another company who moved faster (probably because of their technology advances) and got that candidate instead.

Technology speeds up the timeline for non-traditional (gig) labor by providing a delivery system that enables that worker to start that day, or the next, including on boarding and payments. Technology is also providing a layer of security and safety; in essence it's now become a bit of a truth teller. For many on-demand workforce platforms for independent consultants and freelancers, there are algorithms to vet and evaluate this talent, to prove they worked where they said they worked (that is, as I have said before be careful what you put on social media). Blockchain can now prove if you did indeed work at Microsoft and how you did there.

But technology is only as effective as the humans and processes that surround it. Technology is not and has never been a silver bullet. I have been in front of many clients who have implemented a massive HRIIS solution and struggling to integrate it into their culture, workflows and processes, and other technologies these systems touch. I think the challenges are with any implementation, understanding how to define processes and requirements. And a lot of clients have trouble detailing workflow and entity relationships with other systems.

Not enough time is given to the front end of a technology solution; specifically what problems are you trying to solve? What other technology will this system touch and what are the processes that will need to be updated or changed to leverage this technology as intended? Even with gig workforce platforms that are primarily cloud based; a major implementation is not needed, but you do need to know how you will use this workforce and where they are and are not a fit.

I come across clients all the time who have had WorkDay or some other HRIS system implemented but do not have the aftercare/support needed. They don't understand the technology or how to integrate it into their business fully once implemented. I think there is opportunity for the role of an "after care" specialist to provide support post-launch to help them leverage functionality and features and integrate them into their day-to-day life. Sometimes, it's a matter of knowing what to "turn on." In a lot of cases, after implementation is done, the team that does the implementation leaves and the client really doesn't know how to use their new technology.

HR transformation is a priority at a very high level. The organization of the future is a top priority for companies and Technology is leading the charge for that transformation; talent and workforce solutions are a priority. A lot of HR organizations are behind the curve in addressing key enterprise issues, including talent alignment, skill shortages and organizational change.

Most HR organizations are simply too busy fighting fires to get out in front on strategic issues. In many cases, they are in reactive mode, with too much on their plate. If HR is truly going to deliver strategic value to the organizations, it must change this mindset. HR has to find ways to manage more effectively and prioritize its service portfolio, adopt proactive demand management techniques from IT and make headway on transformation and improvements in key talent areas.

Ultimately, execution and simplicity will be the key to leveraging these technology solutions to step into this new world of work and take your business to the next level. The innovative HR leader will be at the helm along with the right technology partners. HR's new role for organizations is about building the business case and driving user adoption for several types of talent and workforce technology platforms that cover the full lifecycle of talent strategy. Everything is changing, and quickly – including the types of technology HR professional's use, the experiences those systems deliver, and the underlying software designs – making many of the traditional HR systems purchased only a decade ago seem out of date.

Some key tips when exploring the different technology options that enable total and gig workforce strategy (aka learned the hard way):

– Get feedback from the business. What are their biggest pain points?

– Include technology and ensure legacy systems and compatibility are covered. You would be surprised how many implementations fail because this step was skipped and someone spent twenty to thirty million dollars on a solution and they didn't understand the integration points with legacy systems, and so on. So many systems have been brought to their knees by this.

– Looking at an iterative approach, based on prioritizing deliverables and challenges can be a solid choice, and less disruptive to an organization. So, the next question is, what do you tackle first?

– Take care of some near-term pain points, such as recruiting, data or retention, to build consensus from the business.

– Hold the providers accountable: get the requirements right. Then make sure they deliver on them.

– Often, HR tech projects can fail – or at least fail to live up to expectations – not because of flawed technology or a lack of good intentions, but because the organization didn't invest in making the change work.

⬚ Go Out to the People Who Are Using HR Technologies. People are ready to embrace some of the efficiencies but they are not ready to have big disruptive changes. And that's normal. Go out into the field and reach out to the people who are using technologies to find out where the pain is. If it's strong enough, they will be committed to a solution. And the second factor is being able to make sure that all these people who are not technically savvy get the right training from the technology providers.

And you need to understand that, with modern, cloud-based HR technologies, the implementation in many ways is never really "done." The initial "go-live" date still can – and should – be recognized and celebrated by the project team and the organizations, but in many ways that milestone is only the first big step in an ongoing process.

The level of adoption and engagement is not keeping up with the technology evolution that is occurring and HR and Talent Acquisition leaders need guidance, across all components of a modern and fluid workforce solution. There is definitely a lot of resistance to change. Technical changes can be seen specifically as threats by employees who envision that their roles within the company will be replaced by a machine or computer that can do the job cheaper or faster, which may be why they are moving away so slowly from low-value tasks.

Really, technology is elevating the role of HR employees, removing transactional activities and enabling the humans to operate at a high level: strategic thinking, planning, and relationships. Untapped talent, human capability and capacity are constrained by spending time doing things that computers can do better.

The investment decisions the organization makes for its HR and Talent technology will impact the company (for good or bad) for many years to come – perhaps even decades. The time is now to think about making the changes necessary from a people, process and technology perspective and to embrace the new normal of work.

Chapter 9: What Will A Future State Organization Look Like From A Workforce Mix?

> *"The future is already here – it's just not evenly distributed. ~William Gibson – The Economist, Dec. 4, 2003.*

That is the crux of this chapter; future state is already here; albeit in pockets, small samples, pilot groups, scattered across multiple organizations.

The term fluid workforce has been put into the mainstream, along with gig worker, side hustle, remote workforce, non-traditional labor, contractor, independent consultant, and freelancer. These terms came into our everyday usage because this nontraditional workforce is becoming more "normal."

An Article in Entrepreneur Magazine; "A Survival Guide to Global Workforce Trends 2019" Dec. 2018 talks about a couple of trends that point to a new world of work.

A peek into the future means multiple and extended careers as we live longer, and shorter employee lifecycles.

So people are having second or even third acts in their careers. It's never too late to go after your passion. Paul Tasner; the CEO and Founder of Pulpworks, after thirty years in manufacturing was fired at sixty-four. He saw an opportunity to have more environmental stewardship. He founded PulpWorks, Inc. in response to a worldwide plastic pollution crisis; common in his industry; polyvinyl chloride (PVC), accounts for 7 billion pounds of landfill annually. To address this, Paul's company designs and manufactures eco-friendly packaging for consumer products. He started Pulpworks at sixty-six and at seventy, he had a successful multimillion dollar company.

Some businesses, instead of trying to keep employees around longer, are reducing turnover costs by embracing the new shorter lifecycle of employees. Businesses that hire for high-turnover seasonal and low-skill jobs are putting more effort into cost-effective on boarding, training and off boarding processes to get the most out of employees while they're still there. Some businesses have shortened the hiring process to a single interview, or done away with interviews entirely. The Entrepreneur Magazine article focuses on employees, but this kind of lifecycle is more conducive to a fluid workforce. Employee centric models would make this kind of flexibility challenging. The article also goes on to mention that organizations are using technology to win the competition for talent. People analytics derived from these integrated systems can improve hiring and employee engagement, increase productivity and improve strategic decision-making.

I think at its core; the future workforce will be more individual centric than at any other time in history. The focus will shift from filling job titles, roles, requirements, to focusing on outcomes, products, and enabling individual skills, talents, and experience in the most effective way possible to get those outcomes.

We are moving away from a command and control relationship between employer and employee, or worker, or "talent" depending on the category of worker we are talking about. Since the Industrial Revolution, there has been a shift of power or maybe a disbursement of power between the "boss" and "the man" (or "the woman"...someday...that will be a common phrase) and the worker. It's no longer enough to give someone a job to expect complete loyalty and quality work.

Today's workforce wants to be respected, allowed to have freedom, and be inspired. They want flexibility to work hours more conducive to their lifestyle, children, and aging parents. Men are taking paternity leave (okay mostly in California but many non-CA states are also allowing this). The point is leading by top-down, fear, dominance, "titles", are losing ground, and being replaced by teams, cooperation and collaboration.

I have a particularly vivid memory of an older hierarchal system when I was working for a well-known entertainment and media company. The company was known for its highly effective, though rather rigid, patriarchal military style culture and cult-like adherence to the norms of that culture. I was a young finance analyst at the time and was having some challenges with my manager who would be considered a "difficult personality" in that he was passive aggressive, misogynist and was often openly hostile towards confident women. The stress was impacting my health. After several frank conversations with him directly that didn't work, I went "over his head" (his words) to his boss, a V.P., well respected female in the company. She was supportive and told me she would address the issue and she did. But I paid for it, for years after, including a couple poor performance reviews (which luckily no one paid attention to...another dinosaur that needs to be retired, do people still read those?), some blatant freezing out at meetings, and a full year of the silent treatment (him maintaining that consistently was a feat in itself). He said "at my level I did not have the right to speak with her." In hindsight, going around him to his boss wasn't the best way to handle the situation but I was young, inexperienced and at wits end to relive the stress of working for this guy. He retired after working for the company for almost thirty years; he never made it beyond middle management, though he desperately wanted to with several failed attempts at promotion. He was brilliant, but did not know how to be a leader or have the self-awareness to address his issues and it cost him. The workforce of tomorrow will not be about "levels" or titles. The workforce of tomorrow would have "ghosted" that manager after the third day and probably left the company for a better role.

Hundreds of leadership books have been written about "servant style" leadership, and how you get better productivity from inspiring rather than commanding and micromanaging your workforce. Organizations are becoming flatter and career tenures are becoming shorter, along with the lifespan of companies. This means that the ways to build, engage, and manage your workforce is undergoing radical changes. It also means training, succession planning, retention strategies will need to undergo major changes as the lifespan of a worker in your organization becomes shorter and more mercurial. This lifespan also lends itself to a more fluid workforce which is enabled by the gig worker; to accommodate gaps in needed skills, to infuse more innovation into an organization, and to provide the intellectual capital needed to get a project done or meet a deliverable. As we move to more outcomes based ways of doing work, a shorter career span at a specific company will be the norm. Permanent and gig workers will make up the workforce "organism" that will be a moving, breathing thing, changing, morphing, constricting and contracting as markets and demands shift, companies change and grow. Holding on to outdated ways of getting work done and trying to leverage older paradigms of sourcing, recruitment, retention of the traditional worker will limit an organization's ability to grow and thrive.

The future state organization will be about focusing on less hierarchal arrangements, and allowing for a more fluid workforce where turnover is organic, expected, anticipated and maybe even encouraged. Organic turnover can be a good thing; to ensure a dynamic environment that encourages innovation, allows for growth and accommodates the way that the next generations want to work today.

How far away are most organizations from adopting this future state? Not as far away as you would think. As we discussed in earlier chapters; many organizations have begun to embrace looking at how work gets done in a different way. Many are routinely hiring an independent consultant, contractor, or outsourcing all or part of a project where in the past they would have focused primarily on getting the work done with a permanent employee.   Organizations are focused on leveraging technology to manage their contingent workforce spend, on boarding, as well as embracing the suite of options around recruiting, retention, and the other strategies we talked about earlier.   So in many ways, this shift has already begun.

The beginnings are there; pockets within organizations that have adopted a new way of getting work done; you see this often in Technology Departments; the talent shortage is such that they have to expand the net as wide as possible to get the talent they need.   Particularly in hot skill sets like AI, Digital, and Cyber Security.   Some of the best talent can only be found in the gig workforce community.   Many organizations that rely on shift workers; retail, restaurants, are leveraging on demand workforce platforms.   Companies like Shiftgig offers nurses on demand; the nurse's sign up and hospitals can log in to select the nurse they need based on profile and ratings and that nurse gets an alert that they have a project.   Or companies like Allwork provide technology platform where retail workers can sign up for different assignments across multiple department stores in their area where store managers can log on and request them. Each worker has a rating from other store managers, and you can even request the worker to take pictures of their floor to show how displays are being managed; the store managers can log in and view these photos remotely. There is also a GPS location tracking component to prove the worker is indeed working on the floor along with a billing and payment feature that makes invoicing and paying these workers seamless (for a fee). The workers also have the flexibility and options to work around their schedules. Students can accommodate a full course load and have a side income, nurses can work when, where, and how they want to. This approach actually reduces negative turnover and no-shows because you are putting control of the workers schedule in their hands. They are more likely to show up and commit when they can work around the other obligations in their life and choose their own schedule.

Where these advancements seem to work best is with a grass roots approach; starting small, with a problem in need of a solution, and bottom up versus top down. After that, adoption can move quickly. The key is simplicity. Most of these gig workforce technology providers mentioned above are subscription and cloud based; and don't require a major implementation. They are easily added alongside other talent supply chain options like staffing providers, independent consultants and so on. Most are self-contained; sourcing, on boarding, invoicing where the biggest challenge is adoption on a wider scale. Many managers using these "outliers" or "rogue" talent supply solutions are reluctant to build a business case for enterprise adoption as they want to fly below the radar, or if they do tackle enterprise wide adoption, they are not prepared for the bureaucratic rigor that accompanies officially adopting a new solution. Yes, paradoxically, it is exactly these internal champions and visionaries that start the change for adopting something new. As organizations get flatter, and networks become more intertwined, the need to have a top down, and bureaucratic decision that takes months, will diminish in favor of speed, innovation, and execution; particularly when it comes to talent and technology. If someone finds a better way to do something and it works, well, then what's stopping them?

The reality is organizations are struggling to keep up with the changes and looking for answers; usually from Human Resources, who struggle to maintain respect and to be seen as strategic partners. As we discussed earlier, the role of the Human Resources professional is changing. Twenty years ago, HR professional's role was to manage risk for the company, hand out performance review policy, address employee complaints (and make sure the company was not at risk for a lawsuit...yes, that's right, HR's first priority is to protect the company, not you, the employee). But times are changing. HR is being tasked with not only more advanced workforce and talent strategy, but leading the charge on finding, implementing and adopting a growing complex list of HRIS, Analytics, and Workforce Technology. Even with Technology and Operations leaders involved, the decision making is falling more and more to HR departments. The challenge that this poses is a relatively new development in the role of HR leaders, and many are struggling to keep up. On top of this, they fight the day to day fires that exist with the older paradigms which include dealing with recruiting challenges, performance policy, and risk management. They are straddling both worlds; the old and the new, and from what I have observed, they are not getting a lot of help and support from the organizations they support.

These changes cannot happen in a vacuum. The outside world and the way we work is rapidly changing; and the inside world; the traditional employment construct is not keeping up. Not because the HR and Talent acquisition leaders are not smart enough or skilled enough. It's because the changes are happening too rapidly and workforce models; recruiting strategy, role description and creation, retention and training that have been in place for over two hundred years, are changing too slowly or not at all.

Education and shifts in thinking happen slowly, particularly in large organizations or government enterprises, where big ships move slowly. I did a speaking engagement for a New York state government agency last year; to talk about how the gig economy is changing the way we work. Many in the room had never heard of the gig economy and were surprised to learn how many companies were relying on non-traditional labor to get work done. Several people came up to me after that talk to find out how they could use more gig workers. They talked about challenges with their current recruiting strategies; how they couldn't hire enough people because the salaries were lower than the private sector. That the government had trouble attracting people because of the perceptions people have working for the government; that it's dull, not "sexy", the actual lack of innovation and "cool" projects. Interestingly enough, I have talked to several consultants who told me the government often "goes outside" when they need more strategic skills, or want to do something innovative. In fact, these consultants said they loved working for the government because they always pay on time, the work is steady and they get to work on interesting projects. The government was actually leveraging the gig workforce in interesting ways but not intentionally or as part of a larger strategic workforce strategy. It's that intentionality that makes the difference. Taking a step back and thinking strategically about how you want to create your workforce; how do you want to get work done, and by whom and what type of worker? Given technology is such a big part of the new world of work, and most government agencies are working on outdated versions of

HR and Procurement technology (or no technology and relying on spreadsheets and other paper trails), maybe making small incremental changes there is a good start. Before that happens however, embracing this new way of how work gets done has to happen at the top, and it needs to be part of the culture and that is the biggest hurdle.

At the core of these changes is embracing a new way of getting work done. And thinking that can happen overnight, particularly in large organizations is not realistic. Even if change is being forced organically because of market shifts, talent shortages, millennials' habits; it will take some time for these larger organizations to make those changes. This is why the bottom up approach; particularly when there are successes to share such as securing high quality talent, cost savings, improved employee morale, reduced negative turnover, faster fill rates for perm and nontraditional roles. Capturing these metrics and showing in a tangible way how the gig economy has "bottom line" impact is how you change an organization's thinking around embracing the gig economy. The bottom line impact affects cost/process efficiency/productivity which are the holy trinity for a corporation's metrics.

The changes begin and start with one central theme; people. The people who participate in the gig economy; some willingly, some by default because they couldn't find work elsewhere. This is about how "the people" are deciding they want to work differently. They are choosing to work this way and corporate entities are trying to catch up. We spoke earlier about possible factors that might have shaped this trend; technology being the connector to make this possible. Market and economic shifts from the Great Recession that were the catalyst for people to rethink about how they want to earn money, how they want to live, where they want to work, how long, and in what way.

I don't believe that big businesses drove this trend to save money, to "screw the people" to "cut costs" (direct quotes I see posted on any controversial article published on the growth of the gig economy). I don't believe big business has that kind of power. I think the power has always been and will always be, with the people. The worker. Who creates, sells, markets, produces the products and services that make up a company. Maybe we are starting to slowly recognize that power; maybe the great recession, the fall of Enron, the scrutiny and fines around data security with silicon valley giants like Google, Facebook, are waking us up to how important "the people" are.

Growing up, I watched my parents work in jobs they didn't love or even like. My mother worked in the deli department at the supermarket, my father worked in manufacturing jobs his whole life. Back in the heyday of the steel industry, he made great money; as much as many white collar professional jobs, but it was hard work. He did it because he had three daughters to feed and clothe (and buy the good conditioner and designer jeans). Back then, that is what you did and you were grateful for a high paying job. This is particularly true of blue collar work; many do it out of necessity, not because they love what they do. White collar is marginally better, depending on what you do. The money and prestige is better, but it's still the same dynamic. The employer provides the steady paycheck that is necessary to sustain your life and your family. You need to keep the employer happy, do a good job, get good reviews, meet your sales numbers, meet deadlines, win the case, keep sick days to a minimum, get product out the door. The power shift has always been subtly or not so subtly in the employer's hands. I think the biggest fundamental change with the gig economy is the power is shifting subtly back to the worker. Maybe at the center of this massive growth of the gig economy is a desire to shift that balance of power; to make the relationship more equal. Why shouldn't it be? Both sides of the equation get something out of the exchange. A company gets to stay in business, a worker or employee has a way to pay for good, clothing, housing, vacations, education, and charity.

Maybe the equation should be more balanced or maybe even shifting more in the employee/worker's favor. You see that today with record low unemployment numbers and the talent shortage. Even with the massive recession that is supposedly set to hit in the next eighteen months, many analysts are saying it will have little impact on employment numbers due to variables driving the low unemployment rates.

So how does that impact what a future state organization will look like? It will be a mix of talent, working remotely, on site, across the globe. Some will be there a few days and some ten years or more. There will be more networks and teams getting work done. Technology will be the connector, the catalyst and enabler of this fluid workforce to work together successfully to ensure growth and prosperity for a company. Contractors, freelancers, independent consultants will no longer be an anomaly or "fill in" until when you can find permanent talent or to take over short term projects. They will be integral to your workforce strategy and a permanent fixture (albeit a moving one) in your total workforce.

The "Fluid" Workforce

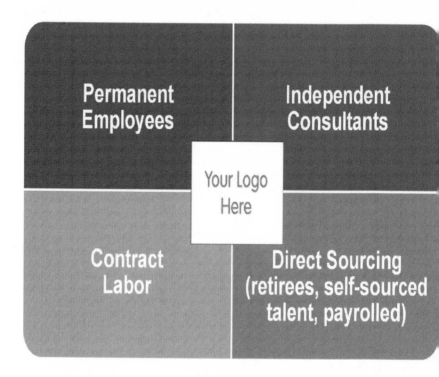

What does this mean for the individual worker? What would their "day in the life" look like in this new normal?

Maybe it's different for each worker in the ecosystem.

Here's an example.

Joe, a Department Head (employee) in New York for a fortune 500 company wakes up, grabs coffee, kisses his wife and heads out the door to the office. He arrives and logs in for quick zoom meeting (with video) at his desk where he receives the latest update on their fifty million dollar project from the Team Lead, Jane, who is an independent consultant based in CA that they on boarded through an on-demand freelancer platform. She's only been on the project for a month and hit the ground running. It's a six month assignment so she has to. Joe takes the update to the conference room where he logs onto a conference call number to bring in the rest of the team, some perm, some contractors, some consultants who are working remotely, from home, or in other countries. The other employees are managers; the V.P. for Technology and V.P. for Marketing are both there, since the project impacts both their departments. They have a great meeting, the project is on track and the ROI from a process and revenue standpoint is substantial.

Joe returns to his desk. He logs into the Vendor Management System (VMS) and sees there are some contractor timesheets he needs to approve for invoicing, and some new resumes of contractors sent to support his now growing team for this project. He approves the timesheets, reviews the resumes and sends a message in the VMS tool to set up interviews for the ones he likes. He then goes to the portal for the on-demand technology provider who gave him Jane, and approves her time. She is thrilled and is paid the next week as she signed up for fast pay option where the on-demand company will provide her money up front (for a small fee) while waiting for the payment from Joe's company, who they will invoice after he approves her time.

Joe has a meeting with their head of Talent Acquisition, Sondra, who is managing the recruiting efforts to find them the ten additional employees they are looking for. She looks up their Applicant Tracking System and sees they have fifteen candidates sourced and vetted for him. He is amazed as he only put the requirement in last week, but their HR department is leveraging a suite of technology solutions; a recruiting network that found them the candidates, that were then put through a video and testing application to ensure they met the criteria, and results were then feed via an integration into Sondra's Applicant Tracking System to let her know who was vetted and still available (as good candidates disappear in this market). She also had some candidates they captured off the company website via a talent cloud technology platform who were directed through the process via bots to ensure they didn't ignore those candidates and lose them to the competition. He is thrilled with her progress and excited about the interviews.

He decides to also log into their talent cloud platform; integrated with their VMS, to see if there are any other candidates he could pick from for contract or permanent work; that "self-selected" to add a profile onto the platform along with their requirements, or worked for his company previously, as a contractor or employee and available again to be redeployed. He found a previous consultant who worked elsewhere in the company that would be a perfect fit. They had a great ranking score, and their previous manager gave good feedback; he called that manager since they work for the same company, and she confirmed, the candidate would be a great hire. He made the suggestion to the Talent Acquisition lead; she was already on it, as she has access to the same system and agrees this would be a good choice.

Joe attends a few more meetings, emails a status update to his boss (who is based in Texas) and is ready to leave. As he does, one of his employees, Lisa stops by to ask if she can work from home over the next few days; she has some personal things to take care of and wants to make sure she sees her daughter 'splay that week. The commute to the office would make that impossible. Joe agrees, Lisa thanks him and takes her laptop off her desk with her.

Joe heads home and decides he will work from home the next day; it's a Friday and most people from his office usually work from home that day anyway. The project is on track, they are meeting the timeline and schedule and C-Suite is pleased. It's been a good day for Joe.

This scenario is not some time in the future; this is very much how many companies are working today in the gig economy. If your company is not, maybe you can show them this chapter, or better yet, give them my number and we would be happy to meet them and build out this strategy for them.

Chapter 10: Freedom To Have Flexibility, Autonomy and Creativity In Your Work – The New Gold Watch

> *To win in the marketplace you must first win in the workplace. ~ Doug Conant.*

The key differentiator for any company to succeed and win is its people, its talent. A company's worth and value in the marketplace is built upon the experience, innovation, drive, work ethic of the people within it. Your Human Capital is the most important investment you can make. We have moved beyond the era of the industrial revolution where you felt grateful for a paycheck and a job. The relationship between employee (and worker) and the employer (end user) has shifted dramatically in this new normal workforce landscape. It is shifting to a more balanced exchange. The talent has more say in the equation and providing a steady paycheck and benefits is no longer the only draw (or even the most powerful draw) for workers today.

As we saw earlier; today's workforce has several options in the how, where and why they work that did not exist twenty-five years ago.

Today's workforce is now incented by different things; they are motivated differently than they were two hundred years ago. Not just at the beginning of their career, but at the end of it. What does that look like and what will it look like in the years to come? What signifies the true end of a career, given so many prolonging retirement and often pursuing their dream to start a business in their fifties, sixties and beyond?

To understand what motivates your workforce, you have to look at the workforce demographic and also at human nature in general.

Demographically, Millennials and Generation Z will make up the majority of workforce. Directly contrasting the preceding baby boomer generation and generations X, millennials and gen z are bringing new skills into the workplace and are seeking more flexibility. They will shape the way businesses build their strategies and recruitment procedures in order to attract and accommodate this new breed of worker. These workers value flexibility and diversity of experience and projects. They want to matter, they want to do work that matters and that has an impact on the world around them. All of these factors are enabled by the gig economy, which makes it a perfect time for organizations to rethink how they engage and inspire their workforce.

One factor to rethink is the concept of "loyalty." There is a perception that exists today, despite these changes, that gig workers are less loyal. They are not as tied to a specific employer or business. Maybe loyalty isn't all it's cracked up to be. Maybe they don't need to be tied to one company for twenty years to be effective and create value. Do you want a worker who is loyal or who produces, is engaged and brings in a fresh perspective and innovation? As company life spans become shorter, and AI replaces jobs, and customer desires and buying habits change on a dime, loyalty may not be as relevant as it was fifty years ago.

The exchange has changed between the worker and the one providing the paycheck. The relationship has become more balanced, and more about mutual positive outcomes. It is no longer enough for an employer to provide a steady paycheck and benefits to attract and retain a workforce. It is no longer enough for the worker to put in a steady eight hours, get good ratings on their performance review and retire after forty years. The equation has changed. If organizations and businesses want to survive and thrive, they will need to accept this fact and make the changes necessary to build a future state workforce. Some have a long way to go.

I was at a HR conference recently; attended by over one hundred and fifty HR professionals, Technology and

Finance executives, to learn about new software trends along with practical tips on leadership, workforce strategy and engagement. I wanted to hear what they had to say, to be a fly on the wall so to speak, and find out what my future potential customers really needed in their talent and workforce strategy.

I was shocked by how many HR leaders still had no idea how dramatically the workforce landscape is changing and some of the questions and frustrations voiced during the breakout sessions was telling. Many are still very much tied to outdated models of attracting, retaining, and sourcing talent. I spoke with a few HR leaders and they said they only used contractors or gig workers "sparingly" because they want to make sure they get "good quality resources" and contractors were not their first choice for prime positions; they would go to "employees." What if the employees didn't want to work that way, what if they wanted to work independently?

Per Spend Matters Enterprises' Use of Contingent Workforce Grows and Business Case is Strong, The Economist's Research Arm Finds ~ March 2019

There are some interesting stats. Specifically when they surveyed respondents (various organizations using or considering using gig workforce) on what the biggest drawback were to using contingent labor, the findings were surprising.

The graph below represents the biggest concerns companies have regarding usage of the gig workforce.

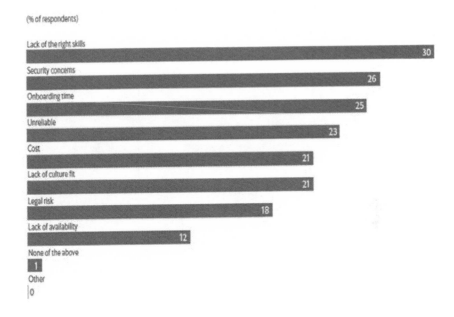

(% of respondents)

Lack of the right skills — 30
Security concerns — 26
Onboarding time — 25
Unreliable — 23
Cost — 21
Lack of culture fit — 21
Legal risk — 18
Lack of availability — 12
None of the above — 1
Other — 0

As the graph indicates, there are still some misperceptions about skills and reliability, though paradoxically, despite these stats, the usage of non-traditional gig workforce continues to grow rapidly today as well as anticipated growth for the future. Per this survey below; 61% of respondents plan on increasing usage of gig workers somewhat or significantly.

So, maybe both sides are starting to come to an understanding; of how the gig economy has changed the way we work, and understanding the value and how this can help companies grow and thrive, and bring a level of agility, innovation and cost effectiveness.

(% of respondents)

Decrease significantly
3

Decrease somewhat
6

Remain the same
30

Increase somewhat
33

Increase significantly
28

Don't know
0

And the main reason this usage will grow is indicated below, when respondents were asked the main benefits of using the gig workforce:

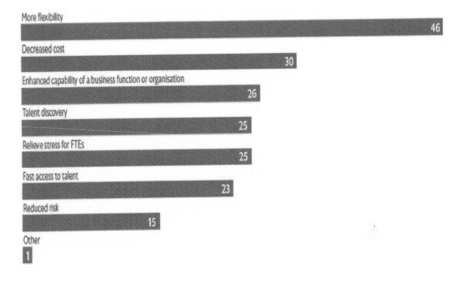

(% of respondents)

More flexibility — 46

Decreased cost — 30

Enhanced capability of a business function or organisation — 26

Talent discovery — 25

Relieve stress for FTEs — 25

Fast access to talent — 23

Reduced risk — 15

Other — 1

So there is a recognition of the benefits to an organization of leveraging this workforce, despite some perceptions (or misperceptions) about the skill sets or reliability of this workforce.

This workforce continues to grow within organizations, even with resistance that may be felt from internal leaders about perceptions of skill and reliability. Maybe that is because the gig workforce itself by its sheer evolution and continued growth is forcing change within companies? This change includes the fact that despite the perceptions of how this workforce will contribute or not contribute, organizations are continuing to embrace and accept this workforce and are slowly beginning to see the benefits a more fluid workforce provides. Ironically, the key benefits enjoyed by both sides of the equation; the gig worker and those that employed them are flexibility; adding to capabilities (by varied experience and projects) and freedom (relieving stress for FTE's).

So we are seeing fewer companies provide pensions, 401K and other long term retirement benefits. Many may see this as companies giving back less, but in reality it is a reflection of the longevity and tastes of the average worker today, as generational differences have an impact on the way we work. Today's worker may not be staying long enough to collect the pension or build up a 401K account. Or as we illustrated in chapter 5, company life spans are shortening as well. So benefits dependent on inherent longevity on both sides have become a thing of the past. How many companies offer 401 matching or pensions today? Most of these types of benefits are only heard of in state and federal agencies; and even those benefits can be impacted by political and economic influences. Even today, few recruiters will even mention these types of benefits as attraction tools, because most workers don't see them as a big draw or even as a true safety net in retirement. Anyone with a fifth grade education can do the math; even with regular contributions and employer matching; by the time one retires and the government take their share of the savings vested; there is very little to live on given inflation. Add this to much longer life spans; the traditional retirement model no longer fits. Most workers are realizing that the value of their skills and experience are better long term investments in the open market hence the explosive growth of solopreneurs and independent consultants, particularly those close to or at retirement age. Reaping the full reward of your intellectual capital and experience is a better long term financial investment than a steady paycheck for many.

So what does today's worker want? What makes them come to work for an organization and once they accept a job (and don't ghost you) what makes them stay?

There have been dozens of books written on this subject. We are inundated with graphs, and diagrams about the "keys to employee engagement" and "defining a culture" and the "top ten reasons employees stay...or leave." There are entire HR Consulting firms that build their service offering around how to change a culture, retain your talent, and revitalize your recruiting strategy; with varying results. Can you really fix a screwed up culture with a graph? Or improve your retention strategy with a couple of team building outings in the Caribbean?

The challenge is many of these concepts and methodologies are based on models that are no longer relevant today. How do you teach recruiting and retention strategies for a workforce that is continually shifting, and moving away from a primarily full time workforce? How will you factor in this shift considering that most of the models historically used were geared towards a permanent, traditional workforce? How do you look at shaping corporate cultures that are impacted by a continuously shifting landscape of workers, many who will not be there beyond a few months? If your people are your company and your culture, how do you embrace the different types of workers, some in your office, some working remotely, some there for twenty-five years, and some there for a six months or one week assignments? Each one of these people is shaping your culture, your products, how your customers are perceiving you. Not all of them want or need a long term role, or healthcare benefits or an annual Christmas party. Some of these traditional benefits are now being trumped by flexibility, remote and work at home options, flexible schedules, generous family leave policies, annual sabbaticals.

One hundred years ago, employees were largely viewed as interchangeable cogs in a machine. One assembly line worker was about as productive as the next. The difference between an outstanding toll collector and a mediocre one wasn't terribly consequential. But in the gig economy, creative and collaborative talents are integral to delivering value. An employee motivated to learn and grow can be much more valuable than a less interested coworker.

So how do you keep your workforce motivated and engaged? Workers today value flexibility, embracing their passion, doing meaningful work; more work life balance (even if this means a lower paycheck). Survey after survey points to money and job stability being a lesser motivator than some of these other options. Time have changed. If you gave the same survey fifty years ago, the focus would have been on a good career, stable company, benefits, pension, and yes, the Gold Watch. (Given mostly to men as they held the majority of the executive roles, but that's another book.)

So how do companies shift to embrace radical changes in the motivations, spirit and heart of their workforce? Your talent is the lifeblood of your organization so how do you keep and motivate your total workforce? Not just your full time employees, but your contractors, independent consultants and others in the gig economy?

Your permanent employees are your core, your culture preservation agents so to speak. They want and appreciate benefits, stability, your time and attention. They also want flexibility and freedom. They are seeing the benefits of working this way, working side by side with a growing gig workforce. That is why so many seasoned executives are now embracing a solopreneur lifestyle and taking some of your clients with them. Yes, even some of your bigger clients, who want to embrace more agile and innovative solutions you can't get from a "Big 4" consulting firm. Maybe enterprise organizations should look at adopting some of those perks for their permanent workforce. Are there ways to expand your work from home policies? Or start one if you don't have one. Having everybody work on site all day, every week is outdated. I was at a party put on by a local co-working space last week and met a commercial real estate executive from one of the biggest financial services company in the world. He was talking about how expensive corporate real estate was to maintain for their workface (several billion in costs annually to be exact) and how frustrated he was by their outdated approach to restricting working from home and other remote working arrangements. It was costly to maintain the real estate and employees resented the lack of flexibility. He mentioned one executive who started an expansive work from home policy that was wildly successful but then cancelled it a year later and "brought everyone back into the office" because top executives had to be sure these employees and contractors were "actually working." Needless to say, shortly after that change, they saw substantial negative impacts due to employee turnover (probably to the competition, which had more progressive remote working policies) and increase in unplanned sick and vacation days to handle child care and other unexpected situations that came up. Situations that could have been mitigated with a little flexibility around where and when these workers got their work done.

There have been many studies done to back up the fact that allowing flexible working arrangements improves employee retention and increases productivity.

I was working with a former client who started her own consulting firm and had a fortune 1000 client in the food services business who was having serious challenges with recruiting processes for their six thousand hourly workforce, all full time; this was their first mistake. This recruiting strategy was costing them two million dollars annually in labor and other costs and it wasn't working. They had negative turnover of over one hundred percent and overworked HR and Recruiting managers trying to keep the talent pipeline full as well as hiring, on boarding and retaining this workforce. The majority were low paying, low skilled jobs and it was hard to find workers with any continuity. So I suggested they embrace the turnover, and fluidity and make it part of their strategy? Um what? I suggested adding temporary workers to the mix, but with a strategy to ensure continuity and performance. I introduced her to an on-demand scheduling and talent pool technology provider called AllWork that provides a platform for retail and other companies with high volume, shift based, low wage hourly workers to maintain their talent pool online, and allow THE WORKERS to select the schedules they wanted to work as well as what location and when. Then the tool's advanced GPS and tracking system would allow the workers to clock in and out online via their mobile phone (with GPS tracking to prove they worked those hours in that location) and the system could also pay these workers via online timesheets. The hiring manger, if they are not in that location, can verify they worked as well as track their performance via online tools like store sales tracking, online photos of location displays and store traffic, etc. There was also a rating capability so if a worker no shows enough times, they are rated out of the tool. The workforce can go through all training and orientation document needed and that is also captured in the technology. They work when they want to which means they are more likely to commit and stay. You have a steady pool of workers (and backup workers) that will take the shifts they want, and keep things flowing smoothly. So now the turnover is an effective part of the strategy and integrated and accommodated into an effective sourcing strategy. The client is now pondering this solution alternative.

Your gig workforce doesn't need the pat on the back (they do that for themselves) but they do want clear direction, to be paid on time, to be treated with respect and to be valued; in fact the respect and being valued applies to all humans, no matter how they are working for you. And yes, an occasional "great job" and "we loved the way you handled that implementation" can go a long way for the independent consultant or contractor who put in seventy work weeks to get that project done on time and under budget.

As someone who has been living and breathing the gig workforce landscape; not only as an entrepreneur but whose team is made up primarily of consultants, I have often faced the question of "how big is your company" and "oh, it's just you then?" The concept of one employee with an ecosystem of highly skilled consultants and experts to deliver is one that is gaining ground slowly, but I often have to explain how this model is just as effective if not more effective than a traditional employee centric company. I have completed large scale projects and initiatives for fortune 500/1000 clients and worked with some of the biggest talent technology and staffing companies in the world. I got these projects and delivered on them with no other full time employees besides myself. I used trusted consultants, who are experts in their field and who have the same commitment and attention to excellence as I do. Some would say this is riskier and less stable than having full time employees. I disagree. Consultants are MORE likely to deliver, be engaged, and do whatever it takes to deliver because there is no tenure or promise of a paycheck. If you don't produce, if you don't keep your skill sets up, you don't eat. My entire business has been built and thrived because of gig workers. My company's logo was designed by the on-line freelancer marketplace Fiverr for twenty dollar. I've used part time contractors to handle back of house operational tasks, my lawyer, accountant, marketing and web design team are all made of independent consultants and small business owners that make Gallagher and Consultants thrive. Without them, I would not be where I am. They are not employees, they don't sit down the hall (or most are not even in the same state) but they have always delivered consistently and with excellence and I trust them, as much as I would trust my own employees. This was more by default than design. When I first started out, I didn't have the money to pay for full time staff and make those commitments but I had to get the work done, so I got resourceful and creative. As the projects and client roster grew, I kept the same approach and it is still working today. Some of the best talents in my industry only want to work this way.

I gave up my addiction to a steady paycheck four years ago. I didn't realize that is what I was doing until I look back now. I worked hard, and produced, and was easily promoted but also experienced a lot of friction and even outright aggression from many of the leaders I reported to. I couldn't figure out why I had such a long string of "bad bosses." I tried hard to fit in, and worked harder when I sensed their growing frustration and discontent with me. I thought something was wrong with me, that I wasn't smart enough, or skilled enough. I always felt like I was doing everything wrong. The stress tore down my body over time. I tried hard to fit in, to make them happy, I worked harder, and it just got worse. I realize now, looking back, like most entrepreneurs I was a really crappy employee. I was outspoken, didn't understand and play within the rules of the terrain (politics), did my own thing, created my own game plan, strategies, and clients loved it but not my team members or leaders. I didn't understand or know how to play within these rules, or be aware of how I was impacting everyone around me, or understand how to make my leaders look good first, be a team player and didn't have enough self-awareness to realize what I was doing and make the changes I needed to make to function within a corporate environment. The friction came because everybody but me saw it. I was just doing what came naturally and felt right and it was not a fit for where I was.

The critical mass finally came when I was fired from a V.P. role at a large staffing and workforce solutions company. A role I fought hard to get and worked my tail off from day one, and tried hard to fit in.

It was the best thing that ever happened to me. My boss at the time was the COO of the company. I have immense gratitude to her for saying what she did; she nailed it. She said "I don't think we are ready for you yet, and I think its best you go out and paint on your own canvas." She was right and as my first firing, it was a gracious one.

She saw what I didn't and she was right. I was devastated; I had never been fired before. I always had an insane work ethic, put myself through college part time while working two jobs. I worked harder than everyone else, came up with new ideas and solutions, bent over backwards to ensure clients were happy. This was the kick in the pants I needed to go out and do what I was born to do, to create progressive, technology forward solutions that helped clients manage their non-traditional labor. (Interesting side note; after I left, three of their top clients that I was managing left shortly after as well, so...maybe there was a method to the madness).

The road after that going out on my own was not easy; there were some dark moments. I was forty-nine when I started, I thought that was probably too old but I did it anyway. Someone once said if you truly want the best self-development program in the world, start your own company, no big ticket conferences needed. You will find out in short order what your strengths and weaknesses are; ego, pride, fear, insecurity, victimhood. You will think you are done with your shit and insecurity, you had the therapy, the spiritual retreats, wine with your best girlfriends, but a whole other level of crap will bubble up you didn't know was there. For the first time in your life you will be forced to deal with your deepest demons and fears. If you don't, you will starve and lose your house. You won't have the confidence to keep hearing no, and running out of money over and over again. You will need to keep moving ahead even though you are terrified, spending weekends alone hammering away at your business, with the occasional glass of really cheap wine. To do this you will need to conquer (or at least make friends with) your demons. There is something about starting your own company, and being center stage, no buffer between you and you, that forces you to shape shift and be a better, strong, humbler, more confident person. That experience is something no one can take from you, whether your business succeeds or fails, it's still worth it because of that. It's worth it because of the person you become in the process; You 2.0.

I wanted to change our industry, create new models of delivering. I hit the ground running. I spent the first six months of my business interviewing former clients to ask what they would have liked to see different, what worked for them and what didn't. I built a trademarked methodology of delivery; **The Workforce Solutions Ecosystem Model** on that feedback. I rolled it out, waiting for the money to come rolling in and year one, after eighteen hours a day and eight hours a day on the weekends, I landed twenty-five thousand dollars in business. I kept going, cashed in my pension, 401K, got rid of activities that weren't serving my business, outsourced some basic tasks, built a better website and got a social media strategy off the ground, got my act together, got my head together, became better, took some sales classes, watched videos. Left my ego at the door. Ran out of money again, sold my house, kept working, selling, delivering, sold my BMW, made fifty thousand dollars my second year. I kept going, and got past the fear and the shit show in my head, and did things imperfectly and made bad decisions, and lived on black beans and rice, and cheap makeup, and ran out of money for rent and electricity and almost got evicted on multiple occasions, but I kept going. I got a lot tougher, more creative, smarter and more assertive; the power of broke will do that to you. I highly recommend it. Most people sitting on ten million dollars in VC capital don't get to hone these skills. Because I KNEW I was on to something. Because I was addicted to the freedom, and creating a company on my own terms, and truly being what I was meant to be and doing what I was meant to do.

I borrowed money from friends and family, it was hard and awkward and I am so grateful to those that said yes (and even those that said no...you kept me going too). I did more speaking, writing, networking, email marketing, cold calls, worked with a sales coach, read and learned more (2-5 books a month) watch podcasts, more videos, on selling, finance, marketing. I got better. I finally wrangled my ego, I became a student. Jim Rohn once said "Don't wish it was easier, wish you were better." To grow my business, I needed to get better, fine tune my approach, listen to customers, and deliver what they wanted better than my competition. I had to break my strategies down, make them more tangible, relatable, and tie them directly to customer's pain in a way they would want to pay for it.

By year four, my company was taking off, and I still like black beans and rice. I eat that every once in a while to remind me where I came from and keep me frosty and on my toes. Plus it's well, just good for you.

My company, Gallagher and Consultants is my "Gold Watch." Like many others in the gig economy; entrepreneurs, solopreneurs, contractors, freelancers, Independent Consultants, the reward system is the freedom, flexibility and autonomy that comes with "being your own boss.'" Actually, this is not true, you have a boss; the client. They are always your boss. And that is the best boss to have. But you get what I am saying. Despite the hardships and challenges that came with building Gallagher and Consultants, there is nothing like it in the world. I wouldn't change a thing.

The workforce of tomorrow is already here on your doorstep. Enterprise organizations must change now, radically, to ensure they embrace this new workforce, and leverage all the benefits and value it brings to both sides. Companies need to create a culture that embraces flexibility, innovation and freedom, whether it's for your permanent or non-traditional workers. That is the secret sauce. These changes are a good thing for both sides. Embrace them and your workers will thrive, produce, and help your company grow; no Gold Watch needed.

Acknowledgements

I could not have completed this book without the insights, exposure, and support of many thought leaders in the gig economy. Many of you probably found yourself quoted in this book, because our conversations shaped the writing of this book, so I hope that's okay. Thank you to Andrew Karpie, at Spend Matters, Subadhra Sriram at Staffing Industry analysts, Noel Cocca at Recruiting Daily, Mike McKerns at HR Insights magazine, and Mark Carrington at Bloomberg BNA, Aubrey Wiete at the Human Capital Institute, and Phil Ideson at the Art of Procurement, who let me publish my crazy ideas in your magazine, and speak on your webinars and podcasts when nobody knew who I was, and giving me the opportunity to add to the dialog in a big way. To Ian Farmer, Mike Keating, and countless others in my network who would also lend your ear for mentorship and advice. To the peers, consultants, entrepreneurs in my network that provided those between the eyes insights at just the right time, or talked me off the ledge, your support and great quotes meant a lot.

I also want to thank all of those people who purchased pre-orders of the book and provided more encouragement than you can possibly know. Thank you for your vote of confidence:

Joan Andrews, Bill Barlow, Dean Bosche, Kanita Brown, Dennis Busel, Alexander Cheng, Mike Cleland, Susan Coschigano, Nancy Curtis, Jeff DerGurahian, Ed DerGurahian, Michael DerGurahian, Coleen Durkee, Noel Dutton, Sheilann Falvey, Trevor Foster, Michele Gibbons, Heather Gourley, Kelly Gouteix, Ken Harris, Jeff Hebert, Brian Hoffmeyer, Jessica Jackel, Don Jackson, Kevin Kiser, George Kroustalis, Gina LaRosa, Jay Lash, Waysoon Lee, Doug Leeby, Jeffrey Leventhal, Jay Mattern, Adela Maynez, Mike McKerns, Roy Medico, Roberta Mee, Chirag Mehta, Vimarsh Mehta, Andrea Myers-Barrilleaux, Chad Nitschke, Mary Painter, Laura Pedersen, Paul Price, Balaji Ramanujam, Carol Reichert, Blake Rhymer, Sean Ring, Lisa Russell, Shashank Saxena, Dan Takah, Michael Wang, Janice Weiner, James Wild, Kip Wright, Brian Wright

This book is about the gig economy and was produced by the Gig Economy; thank you to Fiverr for the editorial support and art work and Amazon books for publishing and printing.

ISBN: 9781695239135

Made in the USA
Lexington, KY
16 December 2019

58600144R10114